FRAGILE AND CONFLICT-AFFECTED SITUATIONS AND SMALL ISLAND DEVELOPING STATES APPROACH

JUNE 2021

ASIAN DEVELOPMENT BANK

 Creative Commons Attribution 3.0 IGO license (CC BY 3.0 IGO)

© 2021 Asian Development Bank
6 ADB Avenue, Mandaluyong City, 1550 Metro Manila, Philippines
Tel +63 2 8632 4444; Fax +63 2 8636 2444
www.adb.org

Some rights reserved. Published in 2021.

ISBN 978-92-9262-904-5 (print); 978-92-9262-905-2 (electronic); 978-92-9262-906-9 (ebook)
Publication Stock No. SPR210202-2
DOI: http://dx.doi.org/10.22617/SPR210202-2

The views expressed in this publication are those of the authors and do not necessarily reflect the views and policies of the Asian Development Bank (ADB) or its Board of Governors or the governments they represent.

ADB does not guarantee the accuracy of the data included in this publication and accepts no responsibility for any consequence of their use. The mention of specific companies or products of manufacturers does not imply that they are endorsed or recommended by ADB in preference to others of a similar nature that are not mentioned.

By making any designation of or reference to a particular territory or geographic area, or by using the term "country" in this document, ADB does not intend to make any judgments as to the legal or other status of any territory or area.

This work is available under the Creative Commons Attribution 3.0 IGO license (CC BY 3.0 IGO) https://creativecommons.org/licenses/by/3.0/igo/. By using the content of this publication, you agree to be bound by the terms of this license. For attribution, translations, adaptations, and permissions, please read the provisions and terms of use at https://www.adb.org/terms-use#openaccess.

This CC license does not apply to non-ADB copyright materials in this publication. If the material is attributed to another source, please contact the copyright owner or publisher of that source for permission to reproduce it. ADB cannot be held liable for any claims that arise as a result of your use of the material.

Please contact pubsmarketing@adb.org if you have questions or comments with respect to content, or if you wish to obtain copyright permission for your intended use that does not fall within these terms, or for permission to use the ADB logo.

Corrigenda to ADB publications may be found at http://www.adb.org/publications/corrigenda.

Notes:
In this publication, "$" refers to United States dollars.

Cover design by Rocilyn Laccay.

All photos are from ADB.

Contents

Tables, Figures, and Boxes — v

Abbreviations — vi

Executive Summary — vii

I. Introduction — 1

II. Background — 2

III. Strategy 2030 Differentiated Approaches — 7
    A. Strategy 2030 Operational Priority Plans — 7
    B. Asian Development Fund 13 — 8
    C. Lessons Learned and Key Operational Imperatives — 10

IV. Enhanced Operational Approaches — 13
    A. Applying Risk-Informed Decision-Making — 13
    B. Improving FCAS Classification Criteria — 14
    C. Assessing Fragility and Resilience — 14
    D. Integrating FCAS and SIDS into Planning and Implementation Processes — 18
    E. Developing Analytics and Knowledge Products — 18
    F. Strengthening ADB's Capacity for Operations in FCAS and SIDS — 19
    G. Expanding Strategic Partnerships and Coordination — 20
    H. Increasing Innovative Private Sector Engagement — 21
    I. Adopting a Communication and Engagement Strategy — 24

V. FCAS and SIDS Approach Action Plan, 2021–2025 — 25
    A. Pillar 1: Improving Responsiveness of Standard ADB Processes, Procedures, and Practices for FCAS and SIDS Differentiated Approaches — 26
    B. Pillar 2: Increasing ADB's Institutional Capacity for Operations in FCAS and SIDS — 27
    C. Pillar 3: Enhancing Understanding of Developing Member Country Contexts — 28

VI. Implementation — 29
    A. Resource Requirements — 29
    B. Interdepartmental FCAS and SIDS Coordination — 31
    C. Strategic Partnerships and Coordination — 32
    D. Results Monitoring Framework and Reporting — 33

Appendixes
1. FCAS and SIDS Approach Links with ADB Operational Priority Plans, and Sector and Thematic Areas — 36
2. Evolution of ADB's FCAS Agenda — 41
3. Asian Development Fund Grant and Concessional Ordinary Capital Resources Lending — 42
4. Problem Analysis — 46
5. Theory of Change and Links to Corporate Results — 48
6. FCAS and SIDS Approach Action Plan 2021–2025 — 52
7. Business Process and Procedure Reform — 59
8. FCAS and SIDS Approach Results Framework — 61

Supplementary Appendixes (available on request)
1. Multilateral Development Banks' Fragility and Conflict Strategies
2. Detailed List of FCAS and SIDS-Related ADB Business Processes, Procedures, and Guidelines

Tables, Figures, and Boxes

TABLES

A3.1	2021 Classification of Developing Member Countries Asian Development Fund 13	43
A3.2	Asian Development Fund 13 Indicative Allocations	45
A7.1	ADB Country-Level Business Processes, Procedures, and Guidelines Changes	59
A7.2	ADB Sector- or Project-Level Business Processes, Procedures, and Guidelines Changes	60

FIGURES

1	ADB's Fragile and Conflict-Affected Situations and Small Island Developing States	3
2	FCAS and SIDS Approach Theory of Change Outline	12
3	Fragility and Conflict Drivers in FCAS and SIDS	15
4	Country-Context Assessments	16
5	Strengthening Project Cycle Responsiveness	17
6	FCAS and SIDS Approach Action Plan 2021–2025 Outline	25
7	Incremental Resources	29
8	FCAS and SIDS Approach Implementation Outline	31
A3	Asian Development Fund 13 Grant Allocation Framework	43

BOXES

1	Understanding the Terminology	6
2	Strategy 2030 Differentiated Approaches to Groups of Countries	9
3	Operationalizing Differentiated Approaches through Fragility and Resilience Assessments	16
4	Identified Changes in Business Processes, Procedures, and Guidelines to Enhance ADB Relevance in FCAS and SIDS	19
5	Partnerships and Cofinancing to Support ADB Green Project Interventions in Pacific Small Island Developing States	21
6	Supporting Essential Infrastructure through the Private Sector	22
7	One ADB (Sovereign and Nonsovereign Operations) Boosting Tonga's Energy Future	23
8	Using Digital Technologies in the Pacific to Offset Remoteness and Limited Resources	26

Abbreviations

ADB	Asian Development Bank
ADF	Asian Development Fund
COL	concessional ordinary capital resources lending
COVID-19	coronavirus disease
CPA	country performance assessment
CPS	country partnership strategy
CSO	civil society organization
DMC	developing member country
DRM	domestic resource mobilization
FCAS	fragile and conflict-affected situations
FRA	fragility and resilience assessment
FSA	FCAS and SIDS approach
GDP	gross domestic product
IED	Independent Evaluation Department
Lao PDR	Lao People's Democratic Republic
MDB	multilateral development bank
OCR	ordinary capital resources
OECD	Organisation for Economic Co-operation and Development
OP	operational priority
PARD	Pacific Regional Department
PPP	public–private partnership
PSW	private sector window
SDCC	Sustainable Development and Climate Change Department
SDG	Sustainable Development Goal
SIDS	small island developing state(s)
TA	technical assistance
TASF	Technical Assistance Special Fund
TOC	theory of change
UN	United Nations

Executive Summary

The paper on the fragile and conflict-affected situations (FCAS) and small island developing states (SIDS) approach (FSA) outlines an operational approach and action plan (2021–2025) for how the Asian Development Bank (ADB) will achieve its Strategy 2030 objectives to improve the effectiveness of ADB assistance and the development outcomes of developing member countries (DMCs) in FCAS and SIDS contexts, and for pockets of fragility and poverty at subnational level.

ADB classifies 11 DMCs as FCAS, and 16 DMCs are SIDS. Afghanistan and Myanmar are classified as FCAS because of ongoing national or subnational conflicts; the Lao People's Democratic Republic (Lao PDR) because of fragility; and 8 of the 16 SIDS (the Federated States of Micronesia, Kiribati, the Marshall Islands, Nauru, Papua New Guinea, Solomon Islands, Timor-Leste, and Tuvalu) because of various dimensions and degrees of fragility. The eight non-FCAS SIDS are the Cook Islands, Fiji, Maldives, Niue, Palau, Samoa, Tonga, and Vanuatu.

Differentiated approaches, based on understanding the causes and drivers of fragility and conflict, and the multidimensional aspects of risk and resilience factors in the specific FCAS and SIDS contexts, are crucial to more productive ADB engagement and DMC outcomes. The FSA will institutionalize ADB's approaches to FCAS and SIDS to improve their development outcomes by

(i) enhancing the flexibility and responsiveness of operational procedures, processes, and guidelines;
(ii) developing fragility and resilience assessments, knowledge analytics, and tools to improve risk-based country partnerships strategies, program planning, and project preparation and implementation in DMCs;
(iii) building institutional capacity for operating in FCAS and SIDS, both within ADB and in DMCs; and
(iv) reinforcing partnerships and coordination.

The FSA utilizes lessons learned from ADB's experience in implementing the 2013 FCAS operational plan and the ADB Pacific Approach, 2016–2020; the results of assessments by ADB's Independent Evaluation Department; and the consultations undertaken with stakeholders to determine how to make ADB's involvement with its FCAS and SIDS DMCs knowledge-driven, context-sensitive, and adaptable in meeting the needs of their populations.

ADB's FCAS team, supported by the FSA interdepartmental working group, led the preparation. This involved extensive consultations with internal and external stakeholders. The two rounds of consultations between September 2020 and March 2021 involved more than 40 different parties and almost 400 participants. They included DMCs, bilateral development agencies, civil society organizations, other international organizations, and multilateral development banks. Internal ADB consultations involved all key departments and thematic groups concerned.

The detailed FSA problem analysis provided the basis for solution development and results analysis, using the theory of change (TOC) method. The TOC method details the underlying activities that differentiate the ADB approaches through three pillars, each with its own outcome— pillar 1: improving responsiveness of standard ADB processes, procedures and practices for FCAS and SIDS differentiated approaches; pillar 2: increasing ADB's institutional capacity for operations in FCAS and SIDS; and pillar 3: enhancing understanding of DMC contexts. The outcomes of the three TOC pillars will be achieved through 13 key action areas supported by 34 sub-actions.

The three TOC pillars form the basis for the FSA Action Plan, 2021–2025, comprising the following operational approaches: (i) applying risk-informed decision-making; (ii) improving FCAS and SIDS classification criteria; (iii) assessing fragility and resilience; (iv) integrating FCAS and SIDS contexts into planning and implementation processes; (v) developing analytics and knowledge products; (vi) strengthening ADB's capacity for operating in FCAS and SIDS; (vii) expanding partnerships and coordination with DMCs, (viii) increasing innovative private sector engagement; and (ix) adopting a communication and engagement strategy.

The fragility and resilience assessments (covering the structural–environmental, institutional, economic, and political–societal drivers) will be part of the diagnostic work undertaken before preparing a country partnership strategy. It will provide a country context-specific analysis of the causes of fragility and propose actions to address fragility and vulnerability, and build resilience. The analysis will be used in country-level planning and updated when relevant, to reflect changes in the country's contextual risk at project level.

The FSA will be implemented by regional departments, through their country programs, with projects prepared, processed, and implemented through sector divisions and resident missions and field offices. Other departments, the Private Sector Operations Department, and safeguard groups will participate in the processing and implementation under the One ADB approach. The Sustainable Development and Climate Change Department's FCAS team will (i) facilitate implementation of the FSA; (ii) provide the knowledge and analytics support, training, tools, and guidance materials to assist these departments as well as DMC counterparts, and help develop skilled FCAS and SIDS staff; and (iii) undertake monitoring and reporting. While some actions will be resource-neutral, others may involve incremental resource inputs. Enhancing capacity will involve training of existing staff and repurposing of vacant staff positions, seeking additional resources based on priorities and Asian Development Fund (ADF) 13 commitments, or through other funding sources.

The FCAS and SIDS coordination mechanisms and working groups will involve cooperation with the sector and thematic groups and operational departments overseeing implementation of Strategy 2030's seven operational priorities' plan and the Operational Plan for Private Sector Operations. In addition, ADB will prioritize strengthening or building regional and country-specific partnerships to improve coordination in FCAS and SIDS.

The results monitoring framework and reporting in FCAS and SIDS will involve a broader set of indicators to assess FSA implementation and performance, including the effectiveness of the FSA in facilitating institutional, behavioral, and procedural changes. These indicators will be based on ADB's existing Corporate Results Framework indicators and tracking indicators, which can be disaggregated for FCAS- and SIDS-specific contexts, and action trackers. The results monitoring framework will provide the basis for the FSA annual report to ADB Management on achievements and performance. ADB will build on existing work in harnessing digital technology applications for monitoring.

ADF 13 and Technical Assistance Special Fund 7 resources were replenished by about $4 billion in 2020 to cover the 4-year period from 2021 to 2024. These are essential funding sources for FCAS and SIDS, most of which are eligible for ADB grants and concessional ordinary capital resources lending. The current ADF country allocation framework for concessional resources will be reviewed to explore options to increase allocations for FCAS and SIDS. The review will include options to incorporate structural fragility and vulnerability into the performance-based allocation formula to increase the share of resources for FCAS and SIDS.

I. Introduction

To achieve a prosperous, inclusive, resilient, and sustainable Asia and the Pacific will require addressing the evolving fragile and conflict-affected situations (FCAS) in developing member countries (DMCs) of the Asian Development Bank (ADB), including small island developing states (SIDS). The objective of the FCAS and SIDS approach (FSA), as outlined in Strategy 2030, is to improve the effectiveness of ADB assistance and DMCs' development outcomes in FCAS- and SIDS-specific contexts, and for fragility and poverty at the subnational level.[1] The FSA puts forward steps to apply context-specific differentiated approaches to addressing fragility and conflict in both FCAS and SIDS.[2] Through implementing the FSA, ADB will develop a better understanding of the causes and drivers of fragility and conflict, as well as the multidimensional aspects of risk and resilience factors in FCAS and SIDS contexts to ensure more productive ADB operational engagement.

Vulnerabilities in the Pacific Islands. Kiribati is one of the small island developing nations that are extremely vulnerable to the effects of climate change, such as rising sea levels.

---

[1] ADB. 2018. *Strategy 2030: Achieving a Prosperous, Inclusive, Resilient, and Sustainable Asia and the Pacific.* Manila.

[2] The FCAS and SIDS linkages are summarized in Strategy 2030 operational plans for Operational Priorities and in the Operational Plan for Private Sector Operations in Appendix 1.

II. Background

FCAS are generally characterized by weak governance and institutional capacity, economic and social insecurity, greater vulnerability to the effects of climate change and natural hazards, and in some cases, political instability.[3] FCAS DMCs include (i) those affected by fragility, defined as a combination of exposure to risk and insufficient coping capacity of the state, system and/or communities to manage, absorb, or mitigate those risks; and (ii) those affected by conflict.[4] Fragility can lead to negative outcomes such as the breakdown of institutions, a deepening of already prevalent societal divisions, displacement, humanitarian crises, or other emergencies and violence. Since 2011, ADB has classified DMCs as FCAS based on the harmonized approach of multilateral development banks (MDBs).[5]

The specific contexts in FCAS DMCs that are affected by conflict are dynamic and may involve insecurity, violence, political instability, and armed insurrection, all of which can arise and change rapidly. Spillover effects from conflict-affected DMCs can also negatively impact the stability of neighboring countries and the wider subregion. The drivers of conflict, particularly in long-term conflict situations, transform economic development and sociocultural practices, and extenuate other fragility factors, and conflict is often concentrated in fragile contexts. While the term FCAS typically refers to a country, it sometimes describes subnational pockets of fragility. In the Asia and Pacific region, subnational conflict is currently the most common type of conflict-related violence.

SIDS are a distinct group of DMCs with specific social, economic, and environmental vulnerabilities, including geographic remoteness and dispersion, small populations and markets, narrowly based economies, low fiscal revenue, high import and export costs for goods, and increasing exposure to natural hazards and climate change.[6] In Asia and the Pacific, SIDS are more affected by extreme fragility that can threaten lives and livelihoods, strain state capacity and service provision, and exacerbate local tensions over scarce land and other resources. The effects of climate change compound these challenges by inducing or forcing migration and internal displacement. Rising sea levels and extreme weather events increasingly threaten SIDS. For the SIDS that are atolls, rising sea levels pose an existential threat.[7] SIDS can be affected by instability or conflict, and several Pacific SIDS have experienced periods of political instability or conflict in the 21st century. Gender inequality as both a cause and consequence of fragility and instability affects FCAS and SIDS, and some Pacific SIDS[8] experience

---

[3] ADB. 2016. *Mapping Fragile and Conflict-Affected Situations in Asia and the Pacific: The ADB Experience.* Manila.

[4] Organisation for Economic Co-operation and Development. 2016. *States of Fragility 2016: Understanding Violence.* Paris.

[5] The MDBs' harmonized FCAS classification system is based on a score (less than 3.2) of the overall average rating of ADB's country performance assessment and the World Bank's country policy and institution assessment, or the presence of a United Nations peacekeeping and/or peacebuilding mission in the previous 3 years.

[6] ADB recognizes SIDS as the collective group represented by the United Nations Office of the High Representative for the Least Developed Countries, Landlocked Developing Countries and Small Island Developing States.

[7] In Asia and the Pacific: Maldives; Kiribati, the Marshall Islands, and Tuvalu.

[8] ADB. 2016. *Gender Statistics for the Pacific and Timor-Leste.* Manila.

a high prevalence of gender-based violence.[9] Many Pacific SIDS share the same structural constraints, though with varying degrees of impact, regardless of whether they are formally classified by ADB as FCAS.

As of December 2020, ADB classifies 11 DMCs as FCAS, and 16 DMCs as SIDS. Afghanistan and Myanmar are classified as FCAS because of ongoing national or subnational conflict. The Lao People's Democratic Republic (Lao PDR) is classified as FCAS because of fragility,[10] and of the 16 SIDS (the Cook Islands, the Federated States of Micronesia, Fiji, Kiribati, Maldives, the Marshall Islands, Nauru, Niue, Palau, Papua New Guinea, Samoa, Solomon Islands, Timor-Leste, Tonga, Tuvalu, and Vanuatu), 8 are classified as FCAS— the Federated States of Micronesia, Kiribati, the Marshall Islands, Nauru, Papua New Guinea, Solomon Islands, Timor-Leste, and Tuvalu—because of various dimensions and degrees of fragility. The DMCs groups are outlined in Figure 1.

The FSA is designed to improve ADB's operational effectiveness in both FCAS and SIDS—despite the differentiated contexts, similarities exist in many of the challenges these countries face and also in the required development responses. ADB responses under the FSA will comprise (i) initiating institutional change, and developing capacity and skills; (ii) revising or developing new ADB processes and procedures to streamline business operations and performance assessment, and increasing flexibility; and (iii) capturing knowledge and creating tools to enhance the development effectiveness in FCAS and SIDS. The FCAS team under the Sustainable Development and Climate Change Department (SDCC) will establish a method to (i) assess the underlying causes and drivers of fragility and conflict when appraising risk and building resilience; and (ii) allow comparison and learning across all ADB-classified FCAS and SIDS.

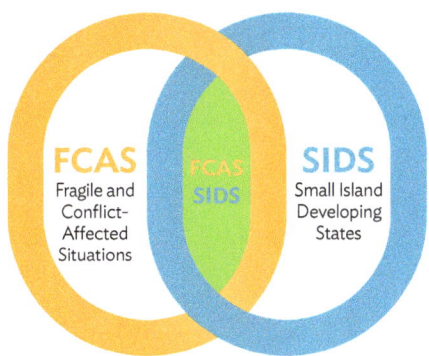

Figure 1: ADB's Fragile and Conflict-Affected Situations and Small Island Developing States

Afghanistan
Lao People's Democratic Republic
Myanmar

Federated States of Micronesia
Kiribati
Marshall Islands
Nauru
Papua New Guinea
Solomon Islands
Timor-Leste
Tuvalu

Cook Islands
Fiji
Maldives
Niue
Palau
Samoa
Tonga
Vanuatu

Source: Asian Development Bank.

In 2013, ADB articulated its approach to engaging with FCAS DMCs through its Operational Plan for Enhancing ADB's Effectiveness in Fragile and Conflict-Affected Situations.[11] The plan was aligned with evolving international practice and detailed actions to mainstream FCAS approaches in ADB country strategies and operations, and encouraged the adoption of FCAS-sensitive internal processes to better address the specific challenges in these DMC contexts.[12] While the plan was well structured and led to the effective execution of some actions in country planning and operations, and more staffing in FCAS resident missions and field offices,[13] it was not fully implemented and experienced resource constraints.

---

[9] Australian Aid Pacific Women. Ending Violence Against Women.

[10] The Lao PDR is experiencing an unprecedented level of macroeconomic stress (including high levels of public debt, and current weak fiscal policy and public financial management), and the coronavirus disease (COVID-19) exacerbated an already fragile economic landscape. As of 2020, major credit rating agencies deemed the country's sovereign credit rating as speculative and of poor standing, with substantial credit risk and default a real possibility. In the third quarter of 2020, Moody's and Fitch announced downgrades to the Lao PDR's sovereign credit rating.

[11] ADB. 2013. *Operational Plan for Enhancing ADB's Effectiveness in Fragile and Conflict-Affected Situations.* Manila.

[12] A comprehensive evolution of ADB's FCAS agenda and the emergence of the global FCAS dialogue is in Appendix 2. The fragility and conflict strategies of other MDBs are outlined in Supplementary Appendix 1.

[13] During 2014–2020, the total number of international and national staff in FCAS and SIDS resident missions and field offices increased from 53 to 86.

ADB's operational engagement with the Pacific SIDS has been guided since 2010 by its Pacific Approach frameworks,[14] while Fiji, Maldives, Papua New Guinea, and Timor-Leste each prepare country partnership strategies (CPSs). ADB is preparing the Pacific Approach for 2021–2025, drawing on the review of the Pacific Approach, 2016–2020 by the Independent Evaluation Department (IED). IED recommended boosting implementation efficiency and the sustainability of impacts by

(i) focusing on alleviating the health and economic crises caused by the coronavirus disease (COVID-19);
(ii) articulating a transformative, differentiated, and FCAS-appropriate approach;
(iii) measuring and monitoring ADB's performance at both the strategic and investment levels, and using evidence to learn, adapt, and demonstrate success;
(iv) working with other development partners for stronger aid coordination and improved absorptive capacity; and
(v) building internal capacity at ADB's Pacific Regional Department (PARD) to deliver and manage the work program and improve coordination with development partners.[15]

Given the susceptibility of SIDS to climate change and disaster risk, the Pacific Approach, 2021–2025 plans to complete a set of climate change and disaster risk management assessments for the 12 Pacific SIDS.

IED's 2019 review of the Asian Development Fund (ADF) XI and 12,[16] **in relation to FCAS and SIDS,** noted that while project performance was lower than the ADB average, it had improved from previous ADF periods. IED recommended that ADB

(i) tailor its systems to match the needs of FCAS and SIDS;
(ii) centralize the FCAS function to support operations, knowledge, and systems;
(iii) adopt targets for FCAS that are differentiated from the corporate targets applying to ordinary capital resources (OCR) operations; and
(iv) enhance monitoring, evaluation, and reporting of results in FCAS and SIDS, while ensuring that enough staff are deployed on the ground.

ADB's comparative advantage as a trusted development partner in FCAS and SIDS is evident in its unique regional perspective of Asia and the Pacific, combined with a growing in-country presence, long-term support and development financing options for the implementation of development programs, and strong client relationships with DMCs. The differentiated approaches under the FSA will be specific to the country context; and the enhanced skills, resources, and capacity of DMCs will help ensure that the delivery of interventions is responsive and adaptable to a changing context. While ADB has focused on infrastructure in supporting DMCs' national priorities, its engagement is broader—covering social sectors (education and health), public financial management, and policy reforms. ADB support in most FCAS and SIDS is financed through the replenishment of the ADF 13 loan and grant facility, and leverages finance (with cofinanciers, and public and private financing), knowledge provision, and key partnerships at regional and national level to facilitate joint work and coordination and thus maximize the development impact for its clients.

FCAS and SIDS have experienced an increase in their populations' fragility and vulnerability because of the COVID-19 pandemic. Rising unemployment (with disproportionate effects on particular social groups such as youth and women), poverty, and food insecurity have exposed the risks that countries face when they have limited capacity and resilience to respond to such exogenous threats. COVID-19 has heightened

---

[14] ADB. 2009. *Pacific Approach, 2010–2014*. Manila; and ADB. 2016. *Pacific Approach, 2016–2020*. Manila. The Pacific Approach, 2021–2025 covers the 12 smallest Pacific DMCs: the Cook Islands, the Federated States of Micronesia, Kiribati, the Marshall Islands, Nauru, Niue, Palau, Samoa, Solomon Islands, Tonga, Tuvalu, and Vanuatu. Niue became the latest ADB member in 2019.

[15] IED. 2020. *Validation of Pacific Approach Country Partnership Strategy Final Review, 2016–2020*. Manila: ADB.

[16] IED. 2019. *Corporate Evaluation. Relevance and Results of Concessional Finance: Asian Development Fund XI and 12*. Manila: ADB.

the existing drivers of fragility and conflict, and compounded the challenges, with expected long-term social, political, economic, debt distress, and environmental impacts.[17] ADB's COVID-19 response proved its ability to rapidly adjust, modify, and streamline business processes under the One ADB approach,[18] given the scale of emergency and the assistance required. An effective implementation of the FSA will require a similar commitment to enable change over the medium term.

Even before the COVID-19 pandemic, while many of ADB DMCs posted a tax-to-gross domestic product (GDP) ratio below the 15% benchmark, which is regarded as the minimum required level for sustainable development, the Pacific recorded a relatively good performance of 21.8%.[19] However, a more granular level of analysis highlights that this performance (based on 2019 figures) is actually skewed reflecting the positive performance of specific SIDS including the Cook Islands (29.0%) and Solomon Islands (23.2%) that have performed rather well, while some of the SIDS such as Papua New Guinea (13.0%) and FCAS such as Afghanistan (8.8%) and the Lao PDR (indicatively estimated at below 11.0%) continue to highlight the intractable issues faced in lifting performance sufficiently for sustained growth.

This performance is expected to further deteriorate because of the COVID-19-related economic downturns, and greater demand for public expenditure, resulting in wider fiscal deficits.

The quantum of impact is varied across FCAS and SIDS, given the importance of different sectors in the respective DMC's GDP. For instance, the Lao PDR estimates the impact of COVID-19 will widen its fiscal deficit from 3.7% to 5.8% of GDP. This widening deficit increases the countries' reliance on limited official development assistance and sources of debt financing.

ADB is supporting FCAS and SIDS in strengthening domestic resource mobilization (DRM), taxation revenue yields, and administration. ADB will provide support to FCAS and SIDS through a regional hub on DRM and international tax cooperation,[20] which will provide an open and inclusive platform for strategy policy dialogue, knowledge sharing, and development collaboration and coordination between ADB's members and development partners. The regional hub will help DMCs, including FCAS and SIDS, define country-specific DRM and international tax cooperation appropriate to their level of development, as well as a revenue strategy and a road map for automated tax administration. The International Tax Pacific Initiative was launched in October 2020, supported by ADB in collaboration with other development partners.[21] This initiative assists Pacific tax administrations in the implementation of international tax standards to enhance tax transparency, prevent tax avoidance, and strengthen DRM in the Pacific region through tailored technical assistance (TA) that is aligned with national strategies and tax administration priorities.

The FSA will institutionalize ADB's FCAS and SIDS approaches by enhancing differentiated operational procedures and processes; developing and applying the findings of fragility and resilience assessments (FRAs), knowledge analytics, and tools; building institutional capacity for operations in FCAS and SIDS;

---

[17] Reliefweb. 2020. *COVID-19 in Fragile Contexts: Reaching Breaking Point.*

[18] One ADB approach supports the multidisciplinary, cross-sector and transnational nature of the challenges Strategy 2030 seeks to resolve. These include (i) public and private sector operations staff working closely together in planning operations, jointly identifying and working on bottlenecks to development results, and processing projects; (ii) integrated solutions incorporating advanced technologies, with support from sector and thematic groups developed; (iii) research functions enhancing the analytical base of operations and policy dialogue with clients; and (iv) staff mobility and recognition through performance management support, as stated in Strategy 2030 (footnote 1).

[19] Source: ADB Asian Development Outlook and Pacific Monitor Economic databases; and ADB. 2020. *Key Indicators for Asia and Pacific,* 2020. Manila.

[20] The establishment of the regional hub was announced by the ADB President at the 53rd Annual Meeting of the ADB Board of Governors on 17 September 2020.

[21] The International Tax Pacific Initiative virtual kickoff event cohosted by ADB, Global Forum, World Bank, Pacific Islands Tax Administrators Association, Australian Taxation Office, and New Zealand Inland Revenue Department, on 14-15 and 20-21 October 2020. This initiative is aimed at supporting efforts of Pacific tax administrations in the phased and tailored implementation of tax integrity standards to enhance transparency, counter tax evasion, and strengthen domestic resource mobilization in the region.

and boosting strategic partnerships and coordination. The FSA will utilize lessons from ADB's experience in implementing the 2013 FCAS operational plan and the Pacific Approach, 2016–2020, the results of IED assessments, and the extensive FSA stakeholder consultations during 2020–2021 to determine how best to make ADB's engagement with its FCAS and SIDS DMCs knowledge-driven, context-sensitive, and adaptable to more effectively meet the needs of populations affected by fragility and conflict.

The terminology used in defining FCAS and SIDS characteristics is outlined in Box 1.

Box 1: Understanding the Terminology

Risk: The likelihood of a threat or hazard occurring, multiplied by the severity of its impact. This is applied to risks associated with different types of threats. For example, risks are identified in relation to disasters, climate, conflict, finance, health, and pandemics. They result from the interaction between the threats and the underlying endogenous and exogenous conditions. Risks can arise from development and project decisions or actions, and from threats external to the development actions.

Conflict: A regional, national, or subnational situation involving armed parties.

Post-conflict: A post-conflict situation refers to a region, country, or subnational area that is emerging from a situation of conflict.

Disaster: A serious disruption of the functioning of a community or a society triggered by geophysical or extreme weather hazard events, leading to human, material, economic, or environmental losses and impacts. Disasters occur when geophysical hazard events (such as earthquakes, tsunamis, and volcanic eruptions) and extreme weather hazard events (such as droughts, floods, and tropical cyclones) interact with the exposure of vulnerable people and assets to those events.[a] A disaster can lead to a state of emergency.

Emergency: A threatening or realized condition that requires urgent action to avoid or address disruption and loss. This includes situations related to food, health, biological, industrial, and technological events.[b]

Displacement: The involuntary movement of individuals as a result of disasters, emergencies, or conflict.[c]

Fragility: A combination of exposure to risk and insufficient coping capacity of the state, system and/or communities to manage, absorb, or mitigate those risks. Fragility can lead to negative outcomes such as violence, breakdown of institutions, displacement, humanitarian crises, or other emergencies.[d]

Vulnerability: Conditions determined by physical, social, economic, and environmental factors or processes that increase the susceptibility of an individual, community, assets, or systems to the impacts of hazards, disasters, and emergencies.[a]

Resilience: The ability of a system, community, or society exposed to hazards to resist, absorb, accommodate, adapt to, transform, and recover from the effects of a hazard in a timely and efficient manner, including through the preservation and restoration of its essential basic structures and functions through risk management.[a]

Resilient development: Enables people, socioeconomic, and environmental systems to cope with a hazardous event or trend or disturbance, responding or reorganizing in ways that maintain their essential function, identity, and structure, while maintaining the capacity for adaptation, learning, and transformation.[e]

Sustainability: The ability of the state, community, or beneficiaries to provide the institutional, technical, financial, and safeguard requirements for the maintenance of systems and processes, and for maintaining the social sector and/or infrastructure investments in the medium-to-long term after the completion of the project or program investment.

Sustainable development: Development that meets the needs of the present without compromising the ability of future generations to meet their own needs.[f]

[a] Adapted from United Nations General Assembly. 2016. *Report of the open-ended intergovernmental expert working group on indicators and terminology relating to disaster risk reduction*. New York.
[b] Adapted from UN General Assembly (footnote e); and United Nations International Strategy for Disaster Risk Reduction (UNISDR). 2009. UNISDR Terminology on Disaster Risk Reduction. Geneva.
[c] Adapted from UN High Commission for Refugees. 2006. UNHCR Master Glossary of Terms. Geneva.
[d] Organisation for Economic Co-operation and Development. 2016. *States of Fragility 2016: Understanding Violence*. Paris.
[e] Intergovernmental Panel on Climate Change: Climate Change 2014.
[f] UN General Assembly. 1987. *Report of the World Commission on Environment and Development: Our common future*. Oslo.

Source: Asian Development Bank.

III. Strategy 2030 Differentiated Approaches

A. Strategy 2030 Operational Priority Plans

ADB's Strategy 2030 calls for differentiated approaches in FCAS, SIDS, and in pockets of fragility and poverty at subnational level to improve development outcomes, including greater diversification of financing products and instruments, and concessional financing support. The details are presented in Box 2.

The FSA implementation will develop and strengthen the links with (i) the seven operational plans for the operational priorities (OPs) under Strategy 2030 and the Operational Plan for Private Sector Operations;[22] (ii) the thematic and sector working groups; and (iii) ADB's ongoing and planned review and reform actions that relate to FCAS and SIDS, such as the Safeguard Policy Statement Review. The seven OPs are as follows:

(i) OP1: Addressing remaining poverty and reducing inequalities;[23]
(ii) OP2: Accelerating progress in gender equality;[24]
(iii) OP3: Tackling climate change, building climate and disaster resilience, and enhancing environmental sustainability;[25]
(iv) OP4: Making cities more livable;[26]
(v) OP5: Promoting rural development and food security;[27]
(vi) OP6: Strengthening governance and institutional capacity;[28] and
(vii) OP7: Fostering regional cooperation and integration.[29]

Each operational plan for the seven OPs and the Operational Plan for Private Sector Operations applies to cross-sector and cross-thematic platforms and defines the links with the differentiated approaches to FCAS, SIDS, and lower, middle, and upper middle-income DMCs. They prioritize ADB support for the poorest and most vulnerable countries in the region, and for lagging areas and pockets of poverty and fragility across all country groups. They also help tailor ADB's business processes and strengthen its human resources and field presence in these countries. They also integrate ADB sector frameworks and policies covering education, energy, finance, health, transport, and water and urban infrastructure and services. The 2004 Disaster and Emergency Assistance Policy and its forthcoming revision provide policy oversight on ADB's engagement during disasters and emergencies, including conflict and post-conflict situations.[30] The FCAS and SIDS links with the operational plans for the OPs and Operational Plan

---

[22] ADB. 2019. *Operational Plan for Private Sector Operations (2019–2024)*. Manila.
[23] ADB. 2019. *Strategy 2030 Operational Plan for Priority 1: Addressing Remaining Poverty and Reducing Inequalities*. Manila.
[24] ADB. 2019. *Strategy 2030 Operational Plan for Priority 2: Accelerating Progress in Gender Equality*. Manila.
[25] ADB. 2019. *Strategy 2030 Operational Plan for Priority 3: Tackling Climate Change, Building Climate and Disaster Resilience, and Enhancing Environmental Sustainability*. Manila.
[26] ADB. 2019. *Strategy 2030 Operational Plan for Priority 4: Making Cities More Livable*. Manila.
[27] ADB. 2019. *Strategy 2030 Operational Plan for Priority 5: Promoting Rural Development and Food Security*. Manila.
[28] ADB. 2019. *Strategy 2030 Operational Plan for Priority 6: Strengthening Governance and Institutional Capacity*. Manila.
[29] ADB. 2019. *Strategy 2030 Operational Plan for Priority 7: Fostering Regional Cooperation and Integration*. Manila.
[30] ADB. 2004. *Disaster and Emergency Assistance Policy*. Manila.

for Private Sector Operations and sector and thematic areas are detailed in Appendix 1.

The FSA will support FCAS and SIDS in building resilience and sustainable outcomes to achieve the Sustainable Development Goals (SDGs). Strategy 2030 and the seven OPs align with and support all 17 SDGs as part of the 2030 Agenda for Sustainable Development.[31] In FCAS and SIDS, several SDGs are markedly off track. The COVID-19 pandemic has had a major impact, significantly reversing most SDG performance achievements.

FSA will require flexibility in CPSs. To effectively leverage complementarities and mutual benefits for FCAS DMCs and SIDS, SDCC will collaborate closely with PARD to ensure that the implementation of the FSA and the Pacific Approach, 2021–2025 will be closely coordinated. SDCC will also coordinate with all regional departments for the preparation and implementation of CPSs for other FCAS and SIDS DMCs.

The FSA will support Strategy 2030's knowledge goals and provide a framework for improved context-specific analysis, including FRAs and associated tools that can be applied under One ADB to more effectively inform the preparation, processing, and implementation of country programs and projects. Strategy 2030 looks to strengthen ADB's country-focused approaches using the CPS as the platform to define customized support, promote the use of innovative technologies, and deliver integrated solutions by combining expertise across a range of sectors and themes and through a mix of public and private sector operations.

B. Asian Development Fund 13

Most FCAS and SIDS are eligible for ADF grant financing, and concessional ordinary capital resources lending (COL).[32] The classification of FCAS and SIDS eligible for ADF 13 grants and COL is detailed in Appendix 3.

Donors agreed during the ADF 13 negotiations on a total replenishment amount of $4,061 million for 2021–2024, which includes an allocation of $3,198 million to ADF grant financing and an allocation of $517 million to the Technical Assistance Special Fund (TASF) 7.[33] Components of the ADF 13 framework relevant to FCAS and SIDS are

(i) a special allocation for Afghanistan;
(ii) an economic vulnerability premium for ADF grant-eligible SIDS;
(iii) the single thematic pool;
(iv) a pilot private sector window (PSW);
(v) an expanded disaster and pandemic response facility; and
(vi) a reserve for changes in debt distress.

The TASF 7 will support group A and B countries in

(i) project preparation and implementation;
(ii) capacity building;
(iii) knowledge generation and innovation;
(iv) debt sustainability; and
(v) policy reforms.[34]

---

[31] United Nations. 2015. *2030 Agenda for Sustainable Development.* New York.

[32] ADB uses a three-tier DMC classification system—groups A, B, and C—based on two criteria: gross national income per capita (Atlas method) and creditworthiness. Group A countries are DMCs lacking creditworthiness. Group B countries are those with limited creditworthiness. Group C countries have adequate creditworthiness and per capita incomes exceeding the operational cut-off of the World Bank's International Development Association (IDA). Access to ADF grants and COL for group A countries is determined by the risk of debt distress. ADF grants are also provided to support specific challenges. Group B countries have access to COL and regular OCR lending. Group C countries have access to regular OCR lending. Refer to Appendix 3, Table A3.1 for funding eligibility of FCAS and SIDS.

[33] The ADF 13 financing requirements also include $346 million for administrative expenses. ADB. *ADF 13 Donors' Report: Tackling the Covid-19 Pandemic and Building a Sustainable and Inclusive Recovery in Line with Strategy 2030.* 2020. Manila.

[34] ADB. 2019. *Seventh Replenishment of the Technical Assistance Special Fund.* Manila.

> **Box 2: Strategy 2030 Differentiated Approaches to Groups of Countries**
>
> **Fragile and conflict-affected situations.** Countries in fragile and conflict-affected situations (FCAS) face a high degree of fragility and a considerable need for institutional strengthening. In countries designated as FCAS, Asian Development Bank (ADB) support will focus on institutional development and governance reforms, essential infrastructure and social services, and targeted social assistance. ADB will support efforts to build resilience, address the underlying causes of conflicts, and promote reconciliation and reconstruction. It will enhance staff skills, tailor its implementation processes to the realities on the ground, and strengthen collaboration with other development partners and civil society organizations to make the country partnership strategies and ADB operations fragility- and conflict-sensitive. ADB will augment resources to accommodate the added costs for processing and supervision because of security and other related needs, and ensure countries that overcome conflict and fragility do not slip back into those conditions.
>
> **Small island developing states.** ADB's Charter gives special attention to the needs of the smaller or less-developed member countries in the region. Small island developing states (SIDS) are particularly vulnerable to climate change and disaster-related shocks. Their rich biodiversity and coastal zones are susceptible to environmental degradation. Their economies are often constrained by small domestic markets, a high cost of doing business, and challenges in connectivity to regional and international markets. SIDS confront severe institutional capacity constraints like FCAS countries. Because of this, many ADB developing member countries (DMCs) classified as FCAS are SIDS, even though conflicts do not pose a dominant risk. They also face a high level of vulnerability to economic shocks, which are further magnified because of their narrow economic base, limited exports, and high dependence on foreign suppliers for many essential goods and services.
>
> Under Strategy 2030, ADB will expand its focus on SIDS (including SIDS that are not categorized as FCAS). ADB's support will focus on climate change adaptation, environmental sustainability, and disaster risk management. ADB will further strengthen connectivity and access in areas like information and communication technology, and sea and air transport; and emphasize institutional strengthening to support countries' efforts to manage financial and economic risks. It will help SIDS improve the business environment, reform state-owned enterprises, enhance public–private partnerships to reduce the costs of doing business, strengthen the quality of public service delivery, and promote private sector-led growth. ADB will continue to tailor its business processes to meet the needs and address constraints in SIDS, enhance hands-on technical capacity building and implementation support, and further strengthen its field presence.
>
> **Pockets of poverty and fragility at the subnational level.** Consistent with its vision to promote inclusiveness, ADB will prioritize support for lagging areas and pockets of poverty in DMCs, including in upper middle-income countries. These areas or segments of the population continue to experience persistent poverty often caused by fragility and conflict at the subnational level. The ADB DMC Graduation Policy provides a framework for country classification based on income, availability of commercial capital flows on reasonable terms, and levels of development of key economic and social institutions. Targeted approaches to address distinct needs in these areas, including through additional technical assistance support and simplified business processes.
>
> **Diversification of the terms of products and instruments.** ADB will conduct a detailed analysis, consultations with stakeholders, and consider using a range of financing terms to implement differentiated approaches that will maximize development impact.
>
> **Concessional finance.** ADB will direct its concessional finance from both concessional ordinary capital resources lending and the Asian Development Fund grant to support ADB's poorest and most vulnerable DMCs. Many FCAS and SIDS are eligible for concessional assistance. ADB will also consider additional support for countries graduating from concessional assistance.
>
> Source: ADB. 2018. *Strategy 2030: Achieving a Prosperous, Inclusive, Resilient, and Sustainable Asia and the Pacific*. Manila.

The volume of ADF grants for FCAS countries during ADF 13 is expected to increase by 12% compared with ADF 12, while TASF 7 support is expected to increase by 50% compared with TASF 6. The volume of ADF grants for SIDS under ADF 13 is expected to increase by about 46% compared with ADF 12, while TASF 7 support for SIDS is expected to increase by 40% from TASF 6.

ADF 13 includes a comprehensive package to enhance public debt sustainability for ADF and COL countries, which will be achieved by

(i) aligning it with the implementation of the International Development Association 19 Sustainable Development Finance Policy;[35]
(ii) rewarding improvements in public financial management with preferential access to the thematic pool; and
(iii) introducing the TASF 7 debt management set-aside to support debt sustainability in ADF and COL countries corresponding to 10% of overall TASF 7 resources ($52 million) during the ADF 13 period.

The debt management set-aside will focus on fiscal, debt, and budget management emphasis in ADF countries at high and moderate risk of debt distress, most of which are FCAS and SIDS.

ADB will review the current ADF country allocation framework for concessional resources to explore options to increase the allocations for FCAS and SIDS. The review will include options to incorporate structural fragility and vulnerability in the formula for performance-based allocation to increase the share of resources for FCAS and SIDS through that system.

C. Lessons Learned and Key Operational Imperatives

Problem Analysis

ADB's portfolio performance and the development outcomes in FCAS and SIDS are lower than ADB's averages. While an overall 70% of ADB operations were successfully completed during 2018–2020, this percentage was lower for SIDS at 56% and for FCAS at 50%.[36] The problem analysis identifies the key constraints and challenges to strengthening ADB portfolio performance and DMCs' development outcomes. It is detailed in Appendix 4 and provides the basis for developing the causal pathways under the theory of change (TOC) process, which is presented in Appendix 5. In summary, the key causes are as follows:

(i) **Inadequate responsiveness of standard ADB processes and procedures to specific FCAS and SIDS needs, contexts, and risks** arising from the incomplete implementation of the 2013 FCAS operational plan. Specifically, this concerns the inadequate assessment of critical drivers and risks in FCAS and SIDS contexts during the planning and implementation processes; insufficient use of existing flexibilities in project design and processing in FCAS and SIDS; inadequate incorporation of necessary flexibility and risk factors in project monitoring and performance evaluation systems; inadequate ADB technical capacity and support; large number of approvals required for processing and implementation; and a low uptake by ADB's Private Sector Operations Department of smaller transactions and higher risks.

(ii) **Inadequate application of knowledge and tools, and limited internal ADB coordination across themes and sectors to respond to the specific contexts of FCAS and SIDS.** Risk assessment tools are not being effectively used and ADB guidelines do not allow enough flexibility to support differentiated approaches to capacity development, project implementation, and project administration in FCAS and SIDS; and a contextual understanding of key stakeholders. Some funding modalities are misaligned with FCAS and SIDS contexts, and the use of multisector, cluster, and umbrella funding modalities for smaller FCAS and SIDS is limited. TA funding is insufficient and disjointed and does not

---

[35] IDA. 2020. *Sustainable Development Finance Policy of the International Development Association.* Washington, DC. The IDA policy involves defining a set of policy actions for ADF and COL countries to boost debt sustainability and assessing progress on their implementation at the end of each year of the ADF 13 cycle. If progress is unsatisfactory, a share of the next indicative annual country allocation will be set aside.

[36] ADB. 2021. *Development Effectiveness Report 2020.* Manila.

support (i) strong knowledge sharing and learning platforms, and (ii) capacity development that is sustainable for executing and implementing agencies, and regulatory bodies (including those concerned with safeguards).

(iii) **ADB institutional capacity constraints**. ADB has limited technical experts adequately trained on FCAS and SIDS operations in the resident missions concerned and field offices, and while staff numbers have increased in resident missions and field offices, some shortfalls in field staffing remain. This is compounded by weak organizational coordination of FCAS and SIDS operations, a lack of incentive structures to retain staff with FCAS and SIDS expertise, and insufficient structured training for ADB staff working in FCAS and SIDS environments. Given these constraints, more technical specialist support is required in key thematic areas, including climate change, gender, and safeguards.

(iv) **DMCs' contextual constraints in FCAS, SIDS, and in pockets of fragility and poverty at subnational level.** ADB has produced limited FCAS- and SIDS-specific analysis on the causes or critical drivers of fragility, risk, and vulnerability; and on factors that limit the building of resilience. Detailed understanding is lacking for the (i) specific contextual constraints (structural, institutional, societal, and economic) in DMCs; (ii) causes or critical drivers of increasing regional, national, subnational, and local fragilities; (iii) factors limiting resilience across FCAS, SIDS, and context-sensitive situations; and (iv) factors limiting the effectiveness of consultations with DMCs, and of country planning, programming, and implementation.

While the problem analysis focuses strongly on ADB planning, processes, procedures, knowledge, tools, and institutional capacity, it also emphasizes the critical importance of understanding the specific contextual constraints of a DMC, and the causes of increasing regional, national, subnational, and local fragilities across FCAS and SIDS, and in pockets of fragility—if ADB's portfolio performance and the development outcomes of DMCs are to improve. The classification of FCAS and SIDS is dynamic, and the causes or critical drivers of fragility, risk, and vulnerability are context specific, classified under structural, institutional, economic, political, and societal drivers. The interaction and interdependence of these drivers in specific contexts generate multidimensional and complex risks. The challenge is how these risks are analyzed in a dynamic environment, managed, and mitigated during the planning, project preparation, and implementation of an ADB country portfolio.

Theory of Change and Action Plan Outline

The TOC is an analytical process to develop solutions and analyze results.[37] The FSA TOC, outlined in Appendix 5, identifies the causal relationships and changes required to achieve enhanced performance of ADB operations, improved implementation by DMCs, and higher levels of development outcomes in FCAS, SIDS, and other pockets of fragility. In the FSA TOC, nine strategic and operational assumptions that operate at different levels provide the basis for the FSA Action Plan, 2021–2025. These assumptions will be monitored regularly, and at least annually, to assess their continuous relevance and adapt them to reflect changes in context. As such, the FSA TOC is both a process and a product.[38]

---

[37] The TOC is an iterative process used to convert problems into solutions based on causal pathways where each action area and result is preceded by its necessary precondition(s). The assumptions are identified in the key areas, from action to result areas.

[38] Ecosystems Services for Poverty Alleviation. 2012. *Theory of Change Manual.* London.

The TOC details the underlying activities differentiating ADB approaches through three pillars, each with its own outcome. These three pillars form the basis of the FSA Action Plan and are outlined in Figure 2 with

(i) pillar 1 improving responsiveness of standard ADB processes, procedures and practices for FCAS and SIDS differentiated approaches;

(ii) pillar 2 increasing ADB's institutional capacity for operations in FCAS and SIDS; and

(iii) pillar 3 enhancing understanding of DMC contexts.

The planned key action areas and defined sub-actions under each pillar represent the steps to achieve the outcomes. These are detailed in section V, and the proposed FSA Action Plan is presented in Appendix 6.

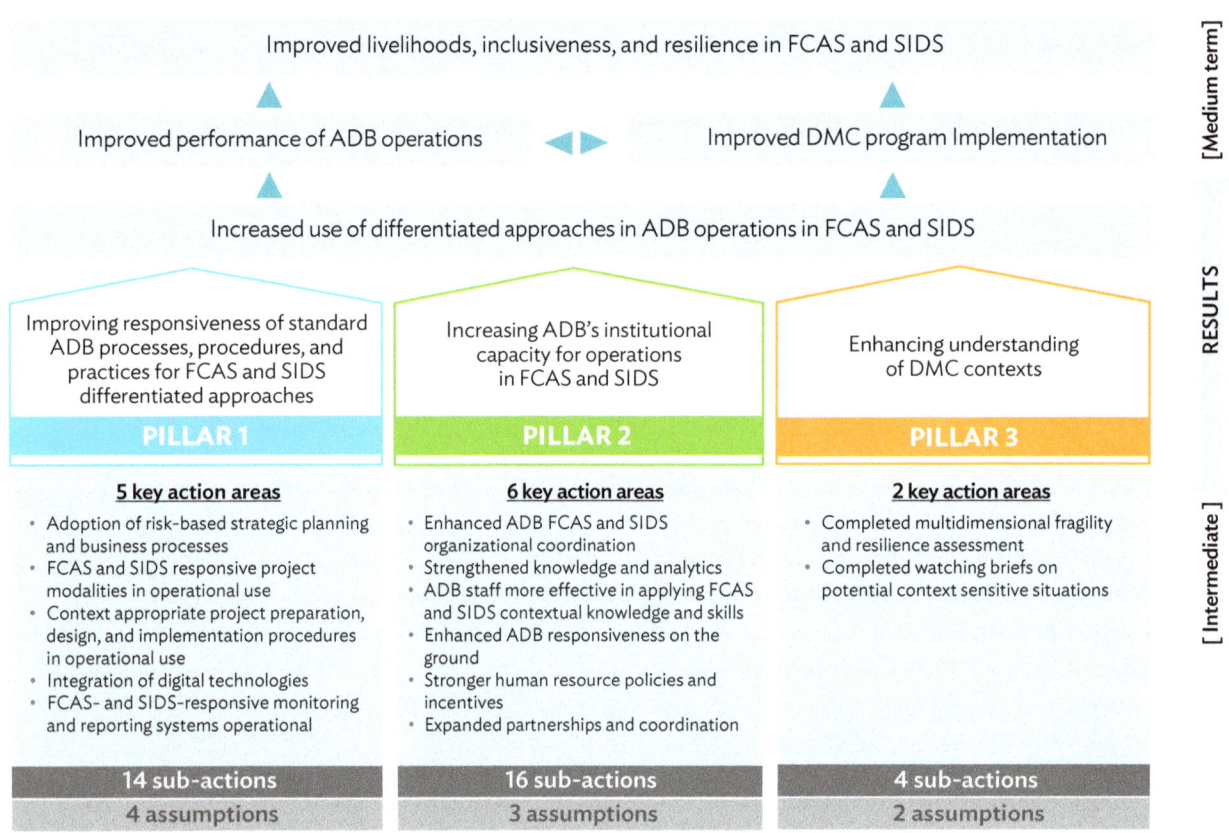

Figure 2: FCAS and SIDS Approach Theory of Change Outline

ADB = Asian Development Bank, DMC = developing member country, FCAS = fragile and conflict-affected situations, SIDS = small island developing states.
Source: ADB.

IV. Enhanced Operational Approaches

The operational approaches of implementing the FSA include

  (i)   applying risk-informed decision-making;
  (ii) improving FCAS classification criteria;
  (iii) assessing fragility and resilience;
  (iv) integrating FCAS and SIDS into planning and implementation processes;
  (v)   developing analytics and knowledge products;
  (vi) strengthening ADB's capacity for operations in FCAS and SIDS;
  (vii) expanding strategic partnerships and coordination;
  (viii) increasing innovative private sector engagement; and
  (ix) adopting a communications and engagement strategy.

A. Applying Risk-Informed Decision-Making

Risk-informed decision-making is the basis for risk-informed development planning; project preparation, and implementation; resilient, inclusive, and sustainable development. Risk-informed decision-making under the FSA will involve (i) analysis, assessment, and understanding of the multiple threats and risks, and opportunities; and (ii) the integration of that risk analysis and the actions required to manage and reduce the risks, opportunities, and associated trade-offs in development plans and programs. It is an iterative process because it requires ongoing review and monitoring as the threats, risks, and opportunity contexts change, and hinges on the flexibility of the planning and project implementation modality to adapt and respond to these changes.

The development of risk-based decision-making frameworks provides essential guidance on development decisions, on the tools and methods for risk assessment, and the resources and capacities required.

Historically, risk management assessments have been treated as a fixed rather than a dynamic variable subject to change, or that the risk focus only addressed thematic risks in isolation. This approach is changing with an increased understanding of the links and multidimensional nature of complex risks and their impact.

ADB, like other strategic partners, has developed risk decision management methodologies and frameworks for project classification, project design (with the design and monitoring framework guidance), public financial management, procurement, climate change, disaster risk management, and conflict. ADB is currently reviewing and updating several such methodologies to integrate international best practices and to be more effective in supporting portfolio planning and implementation under Strategy 2030.

In applying risk-informed decision-making systems in FCAS, SIDS, and pockets of fragility, as outlined in Strategy 2030, a detailed understanding of the specific context (country, subnational, and local) is even more critical given the distinctive characteristics of these DMCs. It is also crucial to ensure that the planned development activities will assist in reducing risks, not generate new risks and increase vulnerabilities, and work to build capacity and resilience, essentially applying a do-no-harm principle. The development context will influence the level of risk tolerance. One element of this reviewing and updating effort is leveraging the risk management work being done across ADB. For example, the sovereign creditworthiness work carried out by the Office of Risk Management to ensure appropriate provisioning of ADB's sovereign portfolio could be leveraged as part of the FSA work. Leveraging these creditworthiness assessments, completed regularly for all DMCs and incorporating inputs from other related departments, would strengthen the consistency of risk management practices across ADB.

Development interventions in FCAS and SIDS contexts will require longer time frames, a focus on quality rather than quantity, in some contexts an increased resource allocation (in processing and implementation), an improved understanding of risks and safeguards, and how to integrate contextual analyses and risk management approaches into design and implementation. Also, as part of the regular portfolio and project review, ADB will refresh and update the context analysis, under existing business processes and project administration procedures, and respond to context changes by adapting or modifying the project scope and project activities. Project designs will need to be flexible; realistic in terms of results to be achieved and able to be modified; and, where feasible, have incremental stages and sequencing of processes and key project activities. At country level, it will be essential to conduct regular and comprehensive portfolio reviews that assess risk context and provide evidence-based information on change and its impact on operations. Ongoing monitoring will be an essential part of the regular review process and, where required, special in-depth reviews will be undertaken if the situation changes to ensure that operations continue to be context specific.

B. Improving FCAS Classification Criteria

ADB has used MDBs' harmonized classification system since 2013 to define a DMC as FCAS. This quantitative system is based on a score (less than 3.2) of the overall rating of ADB's country performance assessments (CPAs), averaged with the World Bank's country policy and institution assessments, or the presence of a United Nations (UN) peacekeeping mission, to delineate FCAS.

The methodology has shortfalls, since the usefulness of a CPA rating as a defining characteristic is limited, particularly in Pacific countries, and because it excludes other forms of conflict, localized situations that emerge in peaceful countries, and the impact on countries from large numbers of refugees from neighboring conflict countries. Many SIDS are fragile in that they face complex disaster risks and/or climate change, economic shocks, and debt sustainability risks, irrespective of their CPA ratings. They are isolated from markets, have very small economies, and limited institutional capacity to sustain public services. Further supplying public services is costly, given the widely scattered geographic spread of the small islands.

ADB is working with other MDBs to develop a new harmonized approach so that it reflects the regional characteristics of fragility and conflict, especially given the distinctive characteristics of the Pacific SIDS. It is expected that the new harmonized approach will be prepared by 2022, after the African Development Bank completes its new strategy for transition countries. As an interim measure for 2021 and 2022, the existing classification system will be followed.

C. Assessing Fragility and Resilience

Fragility and long-term intrastate conflicts have increased regionally and globally, and fragility is also affecting middle-income countries. As indicated in the States of Fragility 2020 report of the Organisation for Economic Co-operation and Development (OECD),[39] a large number of the 57 countries that it currently classifies as fragile are middle-income countries. The underlying causes of long-term fragility are country-context-specific, often complex, and require questioning of the assumptions that countries or contexts can develop their way out of fragility. This raises challenges in development approaches, and an

---

[39] OECD. 2020. *States of Fragility 2020*. Paris.

implicit acceptance of a fragility trap, depending on the critical underlying causes, from

(i) those that are in recovery with declining vulnerability, and building resilience and transitioning to stable situations;
(ii) those that are borderline and transitioning in and out of fragility;
(iii) those that have become fragile because of internal or external causes, or will become fragile because of the effects of climate change and increased frequency of extreme events; to
(iv) those in a long-term fragility trap as a result of climate change, frequent disasters, complex state and socioeconomic causes, or conflict.

This fragility and conflict dynamic and its critical drivers are outlined in Figure 3.

As part of the FSA, fragility and resilience assessments (FRAs) will be undertaken to improve country-level planning and understanding of the country contextual risk.[40] The FRA will be part of the diagnostic analysis that is done in advance of the CPS preparation in FCAS and SIDS.[41] It will integrate all dimensions of fragility (which would link with existing climate change, disaster risk management, governance and corruption, public financial management, and political, conflict, socioeconomic, forced displacement, inequality, gender, and poverty and social dimensions) to provide a broad multidimensional framework for the analysis of links, threats, hazards, risks, vulnerabilities, and resilience. To adopt an analytical approach aligned with the humanitarian–development–peace nexus,[42] the FRA will consider factors of resilience. The parameters of resilience can include having pre-existing economic potential; harnessing a strong civil society, including young people; building on social cohesion

Figure 3: Fragility and Conflict Drivers in FCAS and SIDS

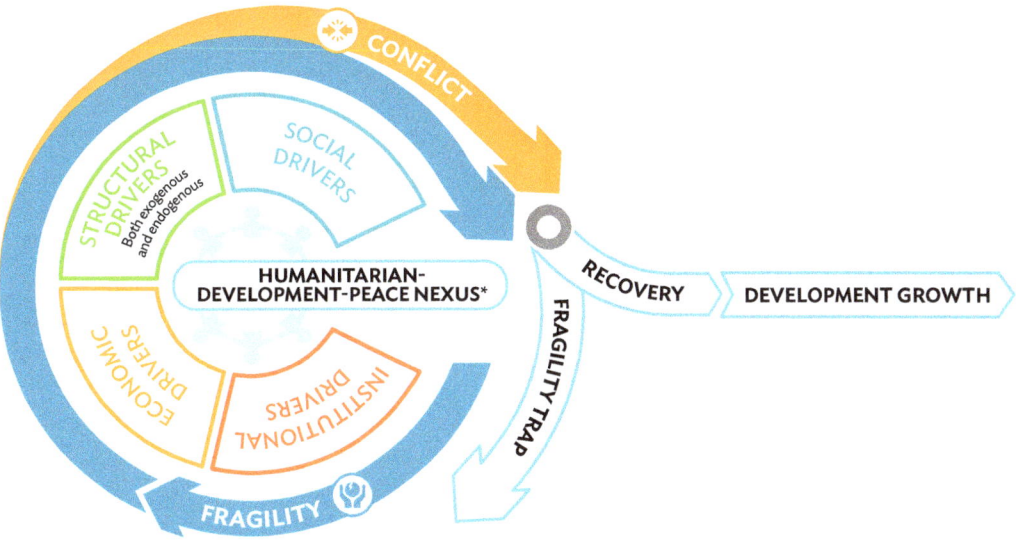

FCAS = fragile and conflict-affected situations, SIDS = small island developing states.

* Organisation for Economic Co-operation and Development (OECD). 2020. Development Assistance Committee (DAC) *Recommendation on the Humanitarian-Development-Peace Nexus*. Paris (OECD/LEGAL/5019).

Source: Asian Development Bank.

---

[40] The terminology used may be subject to change during the guideline preparation.

[41] The ADF 13 commitment is that 60% of FCAS DMCs will have completed a fragility assessment, which will inform the implementation of the existing and the preparation of the new CPSs during the ADF 13 period (2021–2024).

[42] The humanitarian–development–peace nexus is a call for strengthened policy and operational coherence by humanitarian, development, and peace actors, reflecting commitments across key global frameworks such as the SDGs. OECD. 2019. Development Assistance Committee (DAC) *Recommendation on the Humanitarian-Development-Peace Nexus. Paris: OECD Legal Instruments* (OECD/LEGAL/5019).

and coexistence; increasing gender equality; working through local communities; and facilitating international and regional support while recognizing the relevance of trust in public institutions. Figure 4 illustrates how the FRA will be integrated into the CPS.

ADB has carried out FRAs to inform CPS preparations. It recently completed the Papua New Guinea assessment, which was used to inform the new CPS, and work is ongoing on the Afghanistan FRA, which will feed into its CPS for 2021–2025, being prepared in 2021. The process followed in Afghanistan is outlined in Box 3. Under the FSA, a flexible approach and methodology for FRAs will be developed, as well as fragility assessment frameworks that are effective for SIDS and other FCAS contexts, and which will enable comparative analysis across different contexts.

The FRA will use an approach that covers the structural–environmental, institutional, economic, political–societal drivers, and ensures that the core elements are assessed.

Figure 4: Country-Context Assessments

Source: Asian Development Bank.

Box 3: Operationalizing Differentiated Approaches through Fragility and Resilience Assessments

The Asian Development Bank (ADB) undertook a fragility and resilience assessment (FRA) in Afghanistan as part of the diagnostic work in preparation of the country partnership strategy (CPS), 2021–2025. The FRA focused on enhancing ADB's understanding of the country's political, societal, security, economic, institutional, and environmental constraints; and the interaction between such fragility drivers and ADB's sector interventions. The FRA identified institutional, cultural, and socioeconomic factors that act as sources of resilience. Its findings and recommendations provide input into CPS planning and programming, and the design of projects, to make operations more effective, sustainable, and resilient to the changing context, and contribute to improving the country's development outcomes and efforts toward building peace and stability. The multidimensional nature of the FRA required close coordination and synergy with other assessments prepared as part of the Afghanistan CPS process, such as the governance risk assessment, procurement assessment, and sector assessments. Given Afghanistan's high level of political uncertainty, a political risk analysis was conducted to identify critical factors and their potential impact on ADB operations, and to develop management strategies.

The FRA adopted a fully participatory and inclusive approach, including consultations with government agencies, development partners, civil society, and Afghan communities. More than 480 people—45% of them women—were consulted in rural and urban areas across five Afghan provinces; and in each community, engagement was undertaken with a wide range of socioeconomic profiles.

Source: ADB.

The FRA will analyze the causes of fragility and propose actions to manage the fragility and vulnerability, and build resilience. The FRA will be structured so it can be applied and used in planning and processing.

The FRA will be incorporated into the CPS preparation, and the resulting risk-based country programming will facilitate change as the portfolio becomes risk-based, inclusive, and responsive. Applying this in project preparation and design, and updating the FRA with a focus on the particular sector or location context, is expected to result in the adoption of more flexible approaches to risk-based project design and implementation, and adjustments in defining modified scales for disbursement targets based on realistic assessments.[43] Figure 5 illustrates the FRA's critical role in strengthening the project cycle.

The risk-based CPS will also allow for the development of a more robust monitoring system and a broader range of indicators for the country portfolio performance assessment, including fragility and resilience indicators. The FRA includes a political economy assessment; however, a modified approach may be used in a specific context since prior experience in some SIDS has shown that a small population size limits the effectiveness of the political economy assessment. A governance risk assessment and other sector and thematic analyses are also part of the FRA.

The FRA's key findings and causes or drivers, and options to build resilience will be included in the CPS document. The paper on reforming the CPS to align it with Strategy 2030 was approved in 2021.[44] The FRA will be part of the diagnostic work undertaken to inform

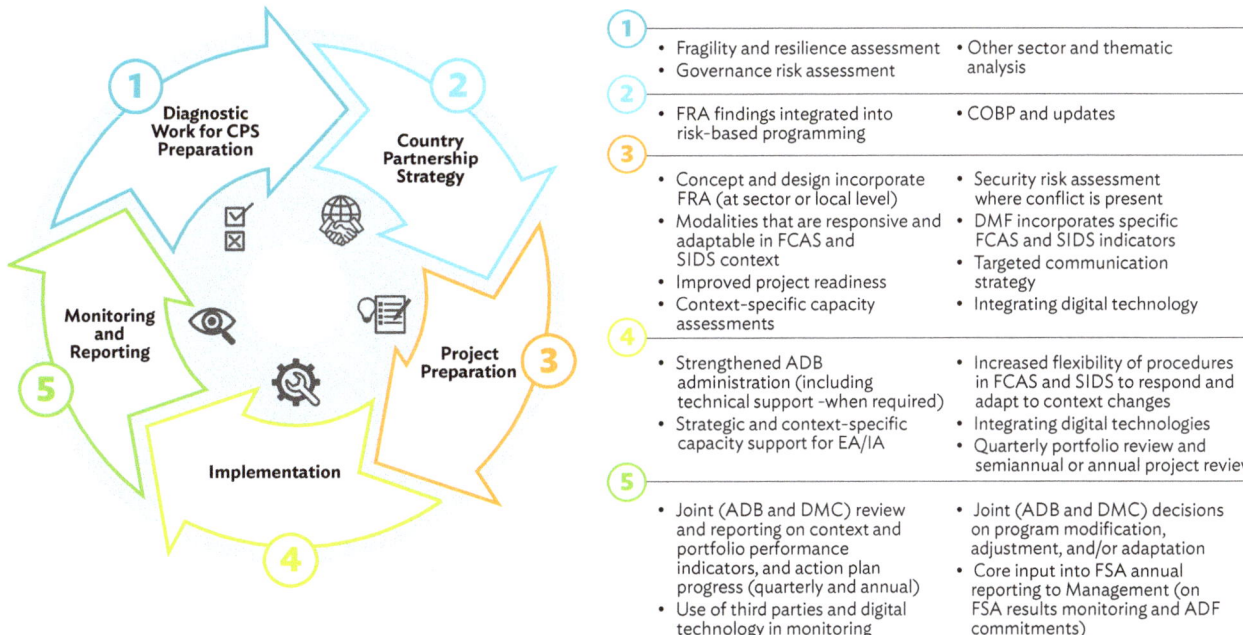

Figure 5: Strengthening Project Cycle Responsiveness

ADB = Asian Development Bank, ADF = Asian Development Fund, COBP = country operations business plan, CPS = country partnership strategy, DMC = developing member country, DMF = design and monitoring framework, EA/IA = executing agency/implementing agency, FCAS = fragile and conflict-affected situations, FRA = fragility and resilience assessment, SIDS = small island developing states.

Source: Asian Development Bank.

---

[43] A revised methodology was adopted for disbursement targets in 2020, using a differentiated approach. It considers the 3-year average of disbursement ratios, country volatility, portfolio size, and balance between corporate and department-level targets, with countries grouped by risk and income status. ADB. 2019. *2019 Annual Portfolio Performance Report*. Manila.

[44] ADB. 2021. *Country Partnership Strategy and Results Framework Review*. Manila.

the preparation for the CPS. The FRA findings will be included as part of the inclusive and sustainable growth assessment, a CPS-linked document.

Tools, training, and resources will be required to develop the FRA, and annual monitoring of progress in FCAS and SIDS will take place. For the FSA implementation to be effective, it will be essential to have trained staff with delegated responsibility in the resident missions and field offices.

D. Integrating FCAS and SIDS into Planning and Implementation Processes

The adoption of differentiated approaches to improve development effectiveness will require the review and revision of ADB's business and implementation processes to ensure that they have the flexibility and responsiveness to support ADB planning, programming, and implementation in FCAS and SIDS environments.

ADB has adopted policies and procedures that guide and support its operations. These are supplemented by guidelines, staff instructions, memorandums, and templates for official documents. Staff instructions set out the business processes under applicable policies and procedures to be followed. While current ADB processes and procedures provide some operational flexibility in application in specific contexts, and new initiatives have been implemented to support FCAS and SIDS, some key areas still require further change, and the development of new approaches.

To more effectively support ADB operations in FCAS and SIDS, the identified priority changes in business processes, procedures, and guidelines include

(i) strengthened preparation of the CPS, specifically by preparing a comprehensive FRA that includes political economy and governance analyses;

(ii) review of the Safeguard Policy Statement (2009) and updates of related guidelines;
(iii) expanded consultation of civil society organizations (CSOs), communities, and youth groups, and their participation at country and project level;
(iv) revised FCAS classification system;
(v) use of existing and/or new procedural flexibility to enhance the processing of sovereign grants and loans;
(vi) streamlined processing of some operations under the Faster Approach to Small Nonsovereign Transactions;
(vii) enhanced procurement and financial management guidance and technical support;
(viii) further guidance and provisions for context-based and tailored project design; and
(ix) development and integration of digital technologies.

Ongoing and planned actions to reform processes and procedures are summarized in Box 4 and detailed in Appendix 7.

A systematic approach that formally recognizes the specific needs of FCAS and SIDS will facilitate and enable the institutionalization and adoption of these procedures. To make this operationally effective will require a change in the mindset among staff working in FCAS and SIDS, as part of ADB's Cultural Transformation Initiative,[45] to ensure context specificity. This will be supported with staff engagement, resources, and training.

E. Developing Analytics and Knowledge Products

Developing and strengthening ADB's FCAS and SIDS analytics and knowledge products will be essential to operationalize risk-based planning, programming, and project implementation. In developing tailored and context-sensitive solutions, the analytical work and knowledge products must be (i) operationally relevant and used to (a) inform

---

[45] ADB's Culture Transformation Initiative aims to improve the way ADB works and foster an environment where staff are empowered and motivated to achieve Strategy 2030 and the shared vision for a prosperous, inclusive, resilient, and sustainable Asia and the Pacific.

> **Box 4: Identified Changes in Business Processes, Procedures, and Guidelines to Enhance ADB Relevance in FCAS and SIDS**
>
> To more effectively support ADB operations in FCAS and SIDS, the following priority changes in business processes, procedures, and guidelines have been identified.
>
> **Staff instructions.** Issuance of new or updated staff instructions to strengthen and streamline business processes for (i) CPS preparation—including a high-quality FRA as part of the diagnostic work to inform the CPS, and integration of FRA findings in project design and preparation; (ii) expanded consultation with civil society organizations at country and project level; (iii) processing of sovereign grants and loans to clarify procedural flexibility and requirements; and (iv) processing of smaller operations under Faster Approach to Small Nonsovereign Transactions.
>
> **Memorandum on FCAS classification system.** Completion of due diligence and analytical work as a basis for preparing an in-depth assessment and filing of an official memorandum outlining an evidence-based FCAS classification system that reflects regional dimensions and SIDS characteristics.
>
> **Guidelines.** Issuance of new or updated guidance notes to inform, clarify, and strengthen technical support for (i) CPS preparation, (ii) FRA preparation, (iii) PEAs, (iv) GRAs, (v) processing of sovereign grants and loans, (vi) procurement, (vii) safeguards, and (viii) development and integration of digital technologies that support country and project performance monitoring, including third-party independent monitoring.
>
> **CPS and project document templates.** Issuance of new or updated CPS and project document templates, including guidance on preparing the (i) CPS, (ii) ISGA, (iii) FRA, (iv) PEA, (v) GRA, (vi) context-based capacity assessment with support plan (included as an optional supplementary linked document of the RRP), and (vii) tailored PAM as an annex of the RRP.
>
> ADB = Asian Development Bank, CPS = country partnership strategy, FCAS = fragile and conflict-affected situations, FRA = fragility and resilience assessment, FSA = FCAS and SIDS approach, GRA = governance risks assessment, ISGA = inclusive and sustainable growth assessment, PAM = project administration manual, PEA = political economy assessment, RRP = report and recommendation of the President, SIDS = small island developing states.
> Source: ADB.

internal ADB discussions with ADB Management and staff, and (b) generate institutional and DMC ownership; (ii) easily accessible both internally and externally; and (iii) supportive of the continued development of a risk-based analytical culture. The FSA knowledge products will align with the ADB Knowledge Management Action Plan[46] and, at country level, CPS country knowledge plan. Knowledge sharing and strategic opportunities for partnerships and joint work will be promoted and facilitated with MDBs, bilateral and UN agencies, other development organizations, international nongovernment organizations, and research institutions. Knowledge sharing will be a particular focus at country level.

To implement the FSA, an analytic needs assessment will be undertaken to verify whether existing knowledge and analytical systems and processes are sufficient. Based on this assessment, a detailed analytics and knowledge framework will be prepared for implementation, which defines the required datasets, tools, and methods for risk and procurement assessments, as well as financial tool kits and guidelines to ensure robust data collection, use, and reporting.

F. Strengthening ADB's Capacity for Operations in FCAS and SIDS

ADB's prior experience shows that effective implementation of a targeted approach in FCAS and SIDS requires commitment at strategic and operational levels to facilitate the institutional, cultural, and behavioral changes associated with the adoption of a differentiated FSA. It takes ownership by the respective operations departments and

---

[46] ADB. 2021. *Knowledge Management Action Plan 2021–2025*. Manila.

adequate staffing with skilled personnel to provide the necessary in-field and hands-on technical and operational presence to support FCAS and SIDS activities. This means providing incentives for human resource development; hiring and retaining skilled specialists; and ensuring that the analyses and tools prepared for the FSA are properly used, implemented, and monitored. Given ADB's institutional constraints on incremental staff positions and its staff resources, especially in regional departments, this may involve training of existing staff and repurposing of vacant staff positions.

ADB recognizes that working in FCAS and SIDS contexts requires a differentiated set of skills and approaches to successfully program, design, implement, and complete projects; to help improve governance; and to do business in these environments. In Strategy 2030, the vision is to adapt and develop learning resources that will strengthen ADB staff's abilities and capacities to successfully manage the challenges when working in these contexts.

In 2020 and early 2021, SDCC assessed the training needs of ADB staff to identify core skills, knowledge areas, and approaches that would be most effective for staff operating in FCAS and SIDS, and also support country partners and the management of critical issues. It is expected that this will require adapted, differentiated, and strengthened courses and materials, and that the learning opportunities for staff will be made available through either formal or informal training. Such training may range from the basic understanding of FCAS and SIDS contexts by applying an FCAS and SIDS perspective to current learning programs, to the possible development and rollout of stand-alone fundamental courses that impart the key skills required for analyzing FCAS and SIDS, designing projects, and implementing operations in these contexts. It is anticipated that this training will be coordinated and prepared in collaboration with regional departments including resident missions and field offices, support departments and sector and thematic groups. Existing fundamental courses, such as financial management and procurement, may be strengthened through targeted case studies and the use of FCAS and SIDS examples. Also, the FSA will explore opportunities to design and implement joint training programs with the sector and thematic groups in implementing some training. This could cover shock-responsive and adaptive social protection, gender-targeted interventions with links between gender and FCAS–SIDS, youth engagement, community-driven development, community contracting, and economic inclusion.

Skill sets will be updated by focusing the training on context-specific application in areas such as stakeholder analysis and engagement, political economy analyses, governance, FRAs, use of risk-based decision-making in FCAS and SIDS programming and project development, delivery of safeguards, and improved awareness of gender-based violence and gender inequality. After the publication of the FSA, a similar training needs assessment will be undertaken with DMC counterparts to define and develop adapted, innovative, and sustainable training solutions for government officials.

Under the ADF 13 Implementation Plan, ADB committed to provide training to 120 staff members to develop a deeper understanding of contextual issues, and differentiated approaches and tools, and to create an online resource center for continuous knowledge dissemination and sharing by the end of 2021. Once trained, these staff will provide a critical knowledge base to facilitate change in operational approaches and processes.

G. Expanding Strategic Partnerships and Coordination

ADB has established strategic partnerships with key bilateral agencies, global and regional MDBs, and other development partners and organizations. They center on fragility, vulnerability, climate change, disaster risk management, conflict and violence, gender equality, displacement, and related social and environmental issues in FCAS DMCs and SIDS. A case study illustrating the effectiveness of partnerships and cofinancing is provided in Box 5. Under the new FSA, ADB will expand its strategic engagement, in particular with bilateral development partners; and promote

> **Box 5: Partnerships and Cofinancing to Support ADB Green Project Interventions in Pacific Small Island Developing States**
>
> **Kiribati.** In 2020, ADB, with cofinancing from the Strategic Climate Fund and from the Government of New Zealand, approved its first project in Kiribati's energy sector. It will increase the share of renewable energy in the South Tarawa grid from 9% to 44%.[a] The project will thus improve energy security, increase grid reliability, and reduce the cost of producing electricity.
>
> **Palau.** Through the Disaster Resilient Clean Energy Financing project, funded by the Japan Fund for Poverty Reduction, ADB is supporting an affordable loan financing initiative. It enables about 900 low-income households and women borrowers to invest in rooftop solar home systems and solar water heating, which in turn will lower these households' energy expenditures. Disaster Resilient Clean Energy Financing is ADB's first financial intermediation initiative in the Pacific. It is being managed by the National Development Bank of Palau. ADB expects to expand and replicate this initiative as a regional financial intermediation instrument covering several Pacific developing member countries.[b]
>
> ADB = Asian Development Bank.
> [a] ADB. Kiribati: South Tarawa Renewable Energy Project.
> [b] ADB. Palau: Disaster Resilient Clean Energy Financing.
> Source: ADB.

global, regional, and country-based opportunities for undertaking FCAS and SIDS analytics and knowledge sharing, training, capacity building for DMC counterparts, and joint assessment work. ADB will also expand its engagement in country partnerships and work with the development coordination bodies of governments as well as working groups to strengthen coordination and coherence on policy dialogue, core strategies and priorities, and with private sector organizations. It will continue to streamline and harmonize processes with development partners, especially given the implementation capacity of government counterparts. As part of this expanding engagement, ADB is participating in key working groups as outlined in section VI.

H. Increasing Innovative Private Sector Engagement

The Operational Plan for Private Sector Operations, 2019–2024 under Strategy 2030 outlines a new approach: an increasing part of ADB's private sector operations would involve investments that are higher-risk, experimental, innovative, and strongly developmental. This higher risk acceptance to be balanced with investments in projects that carry lower risk or generate higher returns to compensate for the higher potential losses. In line with the differentiated approach for FCAS and SIDS, the operational plan outlined an increased focus on poor countries, under-served markets, and expansion into more challenging sectors. It detailed potential areas of engagement in FCAS and SIDS, a need for customized approaches, and the requirement to take on higher levels of risk when financing smaller transactions. Details are provided in Appendix 1. Staff performance assessment indicators have been adjusted to reflect these changes through a mandatory individual performance goal of supporting knowledge sharing, innovation, and collaboration under the One ADB approach.

The shift to private sector engagement in higher-risk contexts with small transactions will benefit FCAS and SIDS and generate economic growth and employment. It will also introduce technology transfer and private sector efficiencies. It requires the use of innovative approaches to financing, guarantees, use of blended finance, and TA to facilitate preparatory stages, and a One ADB approach to combine grants, concessional finance, and TA with private sector lending. The piloting of a private sector window (PSW) under ADF 13 will contribute to reducing some of the shared financing constraints that hinder private sector operations in group A countries, including FCAS and SIDS. The PSW addresses the financing constraints that prevail in many FCAS and SIDS, including (i) lack of access to local currency financing; (ii) limited capacity to carry foreign currency risk; (iii) prohibitive cost of debt capital; (iv) collateral requirements that prevent investors from accessing finance; and (v) limited access to de-risking solutions offered in the market that can improve bankability of borrowers and projects.

The PSW supports private sector operations by helping mobilize, catalyze, and encourage private sector investments through (i) local currency; (ii) blended finance; and (iii) loan guarantee solutions. The PSW is used to encourage and mobilize private sector investment through co-investments and partnerships with other development financial institutions, commercial lenders, and investors for highly developmental projects in group A countries, including FCAS and SIDS. Details are in Appendix 3.

A limited number of small transactions are being undertaken and have demonstrated that for them to work effectively, they require streamlined business processes to support greater uptake of private sector investments, especially small nonsovereign transactions in SIDS and FCAS. Enhancements in the current Faster Approach to Small Nonsovereign Transactions framework are under consideration in 2021. A separate review of existing business processes will also be undertaken. Both measures will facilitate the processing of transactions, including in FCAS and SIDS. Two projects supported with private/public sector financing are outlined in Boxes 6 and 7.

Public–private partnerships (PPPs) are an important procurement modality that can be used for context-specific purposes in FCAS and SIDS. In assessing procurement and funding options for specific types of development interventions, the feasibility of PPPs in that context should be considered. In particular, PPPs can provide the ability to deliver good-quality services efficiently, in the context where the public sector is unable or has limited ability to provide services at such quality and efficiency. Screening potential PPPs at an early stage of planning, using cost–benefit and value-for-money analyses with selection criteria as appropriate, will be important. While the use of PPPs in FCAS has produced some mixed results in some instances in the past with private sector investors, better project preparation and the adoption of legal and regulatory mechanisms will minimize this risk. It is, therefore, important that a PPP legal and regulatory environment exists in the country context, which will enable transparent and competitive PPP procurement methods to be used. Also, the contract design will need to be robust to withstand changing circumstances in FCAS and SIDS environments. Given the limited capacity of SIDS and FCAS to

---

Box 6: Supporting Essential Infrastructure through the Private Sector

ADB is financing Afghanistan's first private sector gas-fired power project.[a] The project will increase domestic power generation and reduce the import of electricity, thereby contributing to Afghanistan's long-term energy security, affordability, and sustainability. The plant, to be built near Mazar-i-Sharif in northern Afghanistan, will use indigenous gas and generate 404 gigawatt-hours of power annually. ADB's Central and West Asia Department funded the project through grants in support of the Afghanistan Power Sector Master Plan, which highlights the use of domestic gas to develop a gas-fired power plant in Sheberghan and two related transmission lines. These will enable the environment for building and operating the facility. ADB Private Sector Operations Department through the Faster Approach to Small Nonsovereign Transactions framework has provided to the operator (i) a loan from ADB's ordinary capital resources; and (ii) the administration of a loan provided by the Leading Asia's Private Infrastructure Fund.[b] It is expected that the project will have a significant demonstration effect for private sector participation in Afghanistan's energy sector.

[a] International Finance Corporation and Deutsche Investitions- und Entwicklungsgesellschaft are cofinancing the project along with the Japan International Cooperation Agency's Leading Asia's Private Infrastructure Fund.
[b] ADB. *Afghanistan: Mazar Gas-Fired Power Project*.

ADB = Asian Development Bank.
Source: ADB.

Box 7: One ADB (Sovereign and Nonsovereign Operations) Boosting Tonga's Energy Future

The landmark Tonga Solar Power Project, currently under construction, is the result of advisory work on an independent power producer tender process from the PSDI and a credit enhancement product developed under PREP. With technical assistance funded by the Pacific Renewable Energy Investment Facility,[a] ADB's PSOD and PARD teamed up to design and develop a credit enhancement structure to support the creditworthiness of power utilities where government guarantees to support their power offtake obligations cannot be given. PREP was successfully launched at the Asia Clean Energy Forum and Pacific Power Conference with great interest from developers and utilities. The solar project, supported by PREP, is helping Tonga step into its renewable energy future. It will rely on a large new battery energy storage system (BESS) on Tongatapu, for which financing was raised by PARD. BESS will ensure that the intermittent electricity generated from solar photovoltaic and wind power developed by the private sector can be stored and used overnight.[b] PSDI provided advisory work to the state-owned Tonga Power Limited on the preparation of the tender process and the drafting of the power purchase agreement. The winning bidder requested PREP support and financing from PSOD, and the project is under construction. The solar project, which was bid to the private sector by a transparent tender process through PSDI, supports a highly competitive tariff to increase energy access, and will achieve effective gender mainstreaming in its operational phase.

[a] The Pacific Renewable Energy Investment Facility finances a series of renewable energy projects in the 11 smaller Pacific island countries (PIC-11). It uses an innovative modality that streamlines ADB's internal procedures, enhancing its ability to process small-value projects in the PIC-11 faster and at lower transaction costs.
[b] ADB. Tonga: Renewable Energy Project.

ADB = Asian Development Bank, PARD = Pacific Regional Department, PREP = Pacific Renewable Energy Program, PSDI = Private Sector Development Initiative, PSOD = Private Sector Operations Department.
Source: ADB.

prepare and tender PPP projects that incorporate international best practices, it is critical that ADB builds the country's PPP institutional, legal, and regulatory capacity and framework through pillars 1 and 2 activities and increases project readiness through transaction advisory services and/or Asia Pacific Project Preparation Funds so that the country can develop and implement a strong PPP program with a robust pipeline of balanced, bankable, and sustainable PPP projects for private sector participation.

In certain projects, a hybrid PPP model may be introduced in which the infrastructure asset is constructed by the public sector, but the operation and maintenance of the asset is done by private sector under the long-term (5 years or more) performance-based operation and maintenance contracts. This will provide an opportunity to introduce the PPP model in FCAS and SIDS, where the public sector and private sector can get experience implementing PPPs in the country in a phased manner and have an opportunity to monitor and build the capacities needed so that comprehensive PPP concessions may be introduced effectively in the future.

Certain PPPs, in sectors that have traditionally been subsidized by government, may run the risk that the services are found to be unaffordable when full cost recovery is sought, either because of the high-risk premiums required by the private capital in this environment or because of the limited ability of the population to pay for the services. The options to address this may encompass support for the use of an appropriate set of risk mitigation and credit enhancement instruments on the private sector side, and with financial viability gap and subsidy mechanisms on the public sector side. In addition, capacity building is likely to be required for the public sector entities to enable them to manage the PPP contract over its entire concession life, including the enforcement of compliance with safeguard requirements. To address any potential negative perceptions of the use of PPPs in FCAS and SIDS environments, ADB should conduct transparent consultations with stakeholders and beneficiaries to explain and detail the potential benefits of using PPPs, and based on stakeholder feedback, incorporate their concerns into the design of the PPP and the accompanying mechanisms, and run a transparent PPP procurement process.

I. Adopting a Communication and Engagement Strategy

A comprehensive FSA communication strategy will support the FSA implementation. The communication strategy will proactively raise FSA awareness and contribute to its institutionalization within ADB and with DMCs and other external stakeholders such as CSOs, civil society, youth, and citizens and development partners. The FSA's success depends on its institutionalization. The communication strategy's core objectives are to

(i) increase the visibility, accurate understanding, and support of the FSA's agenda and objectives by effectively communicating the differentiated approaches;
(ii) strengthen partnerships and activate synergies with internal and external stakeholders;
(iii) disseminate knowledge and share experiences; and
(iv) build trust and a sense of community with stakeholders, especially those in remote and hard-to-reach locations.[47]

Adapted to the unprecedented context defined by the COVID-19 pandemic, the strategy-associated communications plan will adopt a holistic approach and identify target audiences, key messages, mechanisms, and activities to facilitate the dissemination of the FSA content with virtual and digital communications as needed. The plan is organizationally driven and aligned with ADB communication guidelines, will be iterative and provide the necessary flexibility to be adjusted to the evolving context, while ensuring the most effective dialogue with the target audiences.

A preliminary communication plan will support the launch of the FSA. Progressively, a dedicated online resources center will be established. The website, nested within the ADB institutional website, will disseminate FSA related information, FCAS and SIDS knowledge and analytics and cutting-edge research, and promote events and initiatives. A dedicated section will offer training modules to partners (internal ADB's training modules will be hosted in the existing ADB knowledge website). The FSA communication plan includes a variety of products such as blogs, news articles, and other targeted communications media to address FSA information needs of resident missions and field offices. A series of stories, as the "faces of FCAS" will complement the communication initiatives. The communication plan will be evaluated—as part of the FSA monitoring—for its effectiveness in facilitating the desired changes in knowledge and attitudes among the target stakeholders.

---

[47] Stakeholders include all the most vulnerable groups, such as the poor, women, all sexual orientation and gender identities, indigenous peoples, ethnic minorities, persons with disabilities, hard-to-reach and remote populations, migrants, and displaced and conflict-affected people.

V. FCAS and SIDS Approach Action Plan, 2021–2025

The FSA Action Plan is built on three pillars to improve ADB's performance in FCAS and SIDS, and to support DMCs to achieve higher development outcomes and meet SDG targets.

The outline of the FSA Action Plan in Figure 6 illustrates the three pillars and the 13 key action areas, with the 34 supporting sub-actions, covering both existing and new sub-actions. Fifteen are existing sub-actions that cover activities already in progress, or which may require modification, refinement, or a higher priority as part of undertaking current or modified business processes differently. Nineteen are new sub-actions and involve activities that are to be initiated under the action plan.

The detailed FSA Action Plan (Appendix 6) includes information by pillar, key action area and sub-action, implementation timelines, responsible lead and supporting departments, and status as ongoing or new. The delineation by lead department for new and existing sub-actions helps identify areas where incremental resources may be required. Appendix 6 also includes a description of each sub-action.

Figure 6: FCAS and SIDS Approach Action Plan 2021–2025 Outline

PILLAR 1	PILLAR 2	PILLAR 3
Improving responsiveness of standard ADB processes and procedures for FCAS and SIDS differentiated approaches	Increasing ADB's institutional capacity for operations in FCAS and SIDS	Enhancing understanding of DMC contexts
5 KEY ACTION AREA	6 KEY ACTION AREA	2 KEY ACTION AREA
14 SUB-ACTIONS	16 SUB-ACTIONS	4 SUB-ACTIONS
6 NEW / 8 EXISTING	10 NEW / 6 EXISTING	3 NEW / 1 EXISTING

NEW refers to those sub-actions that are to be initiated
EXISTING refers to sub-actions that are in progress, or may require modification (e.g., undertaking existing business processes differently)

ADB = Asian Development Bank, DMC = developing member country, FCAS = fragile and conflict-affected situations, SIDS = small island developing states.
Source: ADB.

A. Pillar 1: Improving Responsiveness of Standard ADB Processes, Procedures and Practices for FCAS and SIDS Differentiated Approaches

The FSA Action Plan will build on existing ADB initiatives, and develop or update processes and procedures as part of an integrated approach to improving operational effectiveness in FCAS and SIDS contexts. This will be achieved through sub-actions in five key action areas.

Key action area 1: Adoption of risk-based strategic planning and business processes. This means

(i) integrating the FRA in the diagnostic work for CPS preparation, in CPS programming, and in the country operations business plan; monitoring context changes (as part of CPS monitoring); and revising programming as required;
(ii) introducing new or revamped business processes, procedures, and guidelines that incorporate flexibility for FCAS and SIDS (Appendix 7);
(iii) streamlining business processes for small nonsovereign transactions; and
(iv) providing technical support to clarify and improve the use and adoption of flexibilities under existing business processes and procedures.

Key action area 2: FCAS- and SIDS-responsive project modalities in operational use. This means (i) broader use of diversified products, instruments, funding modalities (including those under ADF 13), and blended financing; and (ii) greater uptake of smaller nonsovereign transactions.

Key action area 3: Context-appropriate project preparation, design, and implementation procedures in operational use. This means

(i) integrating FRA findings and resilience actions for the specific locational context in project preparation and design; and, for conflict-affected DMCs, regularly updating the security risk assessment (mandatory);
(ii) increasing the use of project readiness financing and small expenditure financing facilities to boost project readiness, especially of larger infrastructure projects;
(iii) increasing the use of alternative and innovative project design and implementation arrangements with stronger project preparation; and
(iv) undertaking capacity assessments of executing and implementing agencies, and preparing a support plan to be incorporated into the project design and related documents.

Box 8: Using Digital Technologies in the Pacific to Offset Remoteness and Limited Resources

Nauru. Under the Sustainable and Climate-Resilient Connectivity Project,[a] drones and digital technology are used to gather and assess data to monitor progress, identify risks and problems, and assist in appropriate responses during construction. They will also be used to evaluate the project's medium- and long-term impacts. Drone technology has proven very valuable for construction supervision and monitoring under coronavirus disease travel restrictions in Pacific small island developing states. The Asian Development Bank has approved technical assistance to design enhanced remote project management tools to overcome the remoteness and limited resources in many of the small Pacific island states. The project is supported by the High-Level Technology Fund.[b]

[a] ADB. Nauru: Sustainable and Climate-Resilient Connectivity Project (formerly Port Development Project).
[b] High-Level Technology (HLT) Fund.
Source: Asian Development Bank.

Key action area 4: Integration of digital technologies. This means support for the development and integration of digital technologies appropriate for FCAS and SIDS contexts (for preparation, implementation, and monitoring) and establishment of integrated digital databases. A case study showing the effectiveness of digital technologies in the Pacific is outlined in Box 8.

Key action area 5: FCAS- and SIDS-responsive monitoring and reporting systems operational. This means

- (i) developing the methodology and performance standards in the FSA results framework;
- (ii) developing and maintaining a dedicated FCAS and SIDS dashboard; and
- (iii) reporting annually to management on FSA achievements and on the performance of FCAS and SIDS as per ADF commitments.

B. Pillar 2: Increasing ADB's Institutional Capacity for Operations in FCAS and SIDS

Implementing the FSA Action Plan will require more institutional capacity on the part of ADB to better handle FCAS and SIDS contexts both strategically and operationally, i.e., to enable the cultural and behavioral changes associated with adopting a differentiated approach, ensure ownership by operations departments, and provide adequate staffing with skilled personnel for the necessary in-field and hands-on technical and operational presence. This will be achieved through sub-actions in six key action areas:

Key action area 1: Enhanced organizational coordination of ADB's operations in FCAS and SIDS. This means

- (i) providing adequate staff (with the required mix of skills and expertise) and resources for the SDCC FCAS team to undertake FSA functions, including application of the FCAS perspective in key areas of operations (themes and sectors);
- (ii) formalizing and operating FCAS and SIDS working groups and networks across themes and sectors;
- (iii) supporting the FCAS anchors across regional departments, and sector and thematic groups;
- (iv) extending existing or preparing new TA projects in DMCs to ensure adequate and consistent support for FCAS and SIDS operations, which includes making use of innovative technologies and providing training to DMCs based on a needs analysis; and
- (v) developing and implementing the FSA communication strategy, plan, and tools to promote and facilitate knowledge sharing and cultural change.

Key action area 2: Strengthened knowledge and analytics. This means

- (i) developing data analytics and tools to support the assessment of geographically-specific fragility, poverty, conflict, and other parameters and classifications; and
- (ii) strengthening analytics and knowledge products based on a needs assessment, and enhancing knowledge management and transfer using ADB knowledge networks.

Key action area 3: ADB staff more effective in applying FCAS and SIDS contextual knowledge and skills. This means

- (i) developing a competency framework, preparing FCAS and SIDS training content based on a needs analysis, and supporting a peer mentoring program;
- (ii) formulating and delivering specific training modules to staff assigned in FCAS and SIDS (ADF 13 commitment), as well as related basic training modules for the ADB induction program; and
- (iii) training ADB staff in institutional capacity development approaches for FCAS and SIDS contexts to support the development of government functions and sustain the transition toward resilience.

Key action area 4: Enhanced ADB responsiveness. This means

(i) strengthening ADB's field presence (resident missions and field offices), and harnessing and pooling cross-regional expertise (sector, thematic, implementation, procurement, financial management, and safeguards); and

(ii) developing contextual terms of reference to attract experienced and motivated staff and/or consultants, and applying specific recruitment strategies for FCAS- and SIDS-experienced international and national consultants.

Key action area 5: Stronger human resource policies and enhanced incentives. This means

(i) using more effective incentive structures to attract and retain staff skilled in FCAS and SIDS contexts;

(ii) raising awareness of the incentive schemes and promoting the mobilization of competent and motivated staff; and

(iii) encouraging further uptake of short-term assignments for national staff in FCAS and SIDS to promote exposure and awareness among sectors and regions, and develop a talent pool.

Key action area 6: Expanded partnerships and coordination. This means

(i) broadening global, regional, and country-specific partnerships and engagement to boost analytics and knowledge sharing, training, capacity building, and joint assessment work in DMCs; and

(ii) increasing coordination with DMCs and development partners on joint programming, funding, and cofinancing opportunities; and

(iii) in conflict-affected DMCs, participating in humanitarian development and peacebuilding forums.

C. Pillar 3: Enhancing Understanding of Developing Member Country Contexts

Implementing the FSA Action Plan will require a detailed understanding of DMC's specific contextual constraints, and the causes of increasing regional, national, subnational, and local fragilities across FCAS, SIDS, and context-sensitive situations. This will be achieved through sub-actions in two key action areas:

Key action area 1: Completed multidimensional fragility and resilience assessment. This means

(i) undertaking an FRA that includes political economy and governance assessments, and integrating the identified drivers of fragility and resilience, and the risk analysis into strategic planning, preparation, processing, and implementation; and

(ii) consulting and engaging with CSOs and nongovernment organizations; women, gender-specific and minority groups (footnote 47); and other relevant beneficiaries, as part of the FRA, on an ongoing basis with regular dialogue and contextual updates.

Key action area 2: Completed watching briefs on potential context-sensitive situations. This means

(i) developing guidelines for maintaining watching briefs on regional, national, and subnational context-sensitive situations, including pockets of fragility and poverty; and

(ii) undertaking watching brief assessments (monitoring using international organization indicators) with risks assessments, and providing briefings to management and operations on potential issues relevant to ADB.

VI. Implementation

A. Resource Requirements

The implementation of the FSA Action Plan, 2021–2025 will require a core FCAS and SIDS team of skilled professionals and trained staff, as well as financial resources, to undertake the planned knowledge products and analytics, training, surveys, studies and reviews, and monitoring and reporting. While some actions will be resource neutral, the overall implementation will involve incremental resource allocation. ADB Management support will be reflected in the President's planning directions, and the Work Program and Budget Framework.

Enhancing capacity for FCAS and SIDS in the SDCC FCAS team and in relevant regional departments will involve an integrated package of resource support that combines strategic use of ADB staff, staff consultants, and TA, especially given ADB's resource constraints and incremental priority demands in other sector and thematic areas—climate change, gender, financial management, and health—and operationally in PARD and the Private Sector Operations Department. As outlined in Figure 7, ADB's capacity enhancement will be achieved with more agile human resource utilization. This means (i) providing staff training, repurposing vacant staff positions, redeploying staff,

Figure 7: Incremental Resources

ADB Staff	• Redeployment of staff
	• Retraining of staff
	• Repurposing of vacant staff positions
	• Fixed-term staff positions
		• Secondments
		• Human resource agility
		   ○ short-term assignments
		   ○ resource pooling across regions

Staff Consultants	• Provide additional resources for staff consultants to jump-start the implementation
	• Support initial surge of activities, such as
	   ○ revision of staff instructions
	   ○ preparation of guidance notes
	   ○ knowledge and analytics
	   ○ capacity development	

Technical Assistance	• Training, capacity building, enhancement and supplementation in DMCs • Ongoing corporate TA with SDCC FCAS	

ADB = Asian Development Bank, DMCs = developing member countries, FCAS = fragile and conflict-affected situations, SDCC = Sustainable Development and Climate Change Department, TA = technical assistance.

Source: ADB.

using fixed-term staff positions and secondments, pooling resources such as key technical skills in hubs across regions, and harnessing resources thematically; (ii) using staff consultants to assist in the expected surge of activities, and support the implementation of key FSA actions after their approval; and (iii) providing TA to DMCs to support training, capacity building, enhancement, and supplementation. In 2020, ADB demonstrated its capacity to rapidly adapt and deliver in a COVID-19-constrained environment by implementing efficient resource allocation changes, which are likely to continue.

The provision of resources as outlined provides the foundation for the FSA's operational effectiveness and long-term sustainability. It will be responsive to the specific regional and technical requirements, given the significant differences across regional departments. While it may be feasible in some departments with few FCAS or SIDS to undertake FSA actions with limited incremental resource inputs, in other departments such as PARD—which includes nearly all of the regional SIDS and a large number of FCAS, and is currently resource constrained— incremental resources will be necessary for effective implementation. In addition, PARD will be processing and administering a larger portfolio with the dedicated funding allocation for SIDS under ADF 13.

The SDCC FCAS team will provide technical support to enhance the responsiveness to FCAS and SIDS contexts, and to increase the institutional capacity for and understanding of DMC-specific contexts. The SDCC FCAS team will collaborate with PARD and other operations departments on these aspects.

The core work tasks of the SDCC FCAS team will cover the

(i) provision of technical support to regional departments with FCAS and SIDS, and the seven OPs and thematic groups;
(ii) preparation of knowledge products, tools, analytics, and training;
(iii) coordination across the related interdepartmental working groups to facilitate uniform adoption and implementation of the FSA; and
(iv) monitoring and reporting FSA progress to ADB Management.

These tasks will require a core team of specialists with expertise in the areas of FCAS and SIDS advisory; fragility and conflict; knowledge products, tools, analytics and training; and monitoring and reporting. To ensure that ADB's corporate FCAS expertise and knowledge is developed and institutionalized, a core set of team members should be ADB staff, and any others either consultants or secondees from development organizations or institutions. For specialist knowledge work, analytics, tools, and studies, short-term consultant inputs are proposed.

In the regional departments with operations in FCAS and SIDS, the core FSA work will cover FRA preparation and integration into the CPS and CPS programming—or, where relevant in SIDS that are part of the Pacific Approach, the use of a modified approach—as part of the diagnostic work, and as an integral element in project processing, implementation management, and portfolio performance monitoring. The tasks will be part of the workplans of the regional departments, with staff responsibilities identified and annual performance assessed.

Regional departments will determine whether to use existing trained staff, or department and/or resident mission- and field office-based technical specialists to provide fragility or conflict inputs into the FRA (which is anticipated to be undertaken with consultant inputs) and integrate into the CPS and related programs. Technical support to the processing teams may involve the use of a fragility or conflict consultant(s), to ensure that location-specific fragility or conflict drivers and resilience contexts are integrated into the project cycle and monitoring systems. Technical support to staff may also be required to facilitate the adoption of risk-based FCAS and SIDS programming and practices, and as part of project and portfolio reviews that involve context change and adaptation. PARD will continue to build operational understanding and experience in FCAS and SIDS environments in all staff. The staffing requirements will depend on the given FCAS and SIDS contexts and complexity.

B. Interdepartmental FCAS and SIDS Coordination

The FSA is a specific part of the overall set of plans—i.e., the seven OPs, the Operational Plan for Private Sector Operations, and thematic and sector plans—that form the basis for implementing Strategy 2030. For this reason, clearly identifying the cross-links between the FSA and the OPs and Operational Plan for Private Sector Operations, and sector frameworks is essential to ensure that coordinated and integrated approaches are applied in FCAS and SIDS. Some OPs have explicitly defined the differentiated FCAS and SIDS actions (Appendix 1).

The FSA actions that are the responsibility of regional departments will be implemented through their country programs, with projects prepared, processed, and implemented through sector divisions and resident missions or field offices. The supporting departments (including those concerned with private sector operations) and safeguard staff will participate in the processing and implementation under One ADB. The SDCC FCAS team will promote FSA best adapted practices; provide the knowledge and analytics support, training, tools, and guidance materials to support these departments; and support the development of a cadre of skilled FCAS and SIDS staff. The SDCC FCAS team and SIDS technical experts will serve as members on ADB's key policy, thematic, operational, and procedural working groups. Figure 8 outlines the specific roles that ADB and its DMC counterparts will undertake in institutionalizing the FSA.

The ADB-internal links to implement the FSA will involve structured institutional arrangements on FCAS and SIDS coordination mechanisms and working groups, with defined responsibilities. This is currently being developed.

Figure 8: FCAS and SIDS Approach Implementation Outline

OPERATIONS DEPARTMENT

Country team:
- Diagnostic work for CPS– FRA, GRA, etc. => ISGA
  - Opportunities for joint analytical work with development partners
- CPS annual reporting performance monitoring (new CPS)
- Portfolio review monitoring and actions to respond and adapt to context changes

Project teams:
- Preparation and design (for specific context fragility and resilience) using responsive modalities, readiness indicators and implementation (sovereign and nonsovereign)

Training and capacity development
- Trained skilled staff (RD, RM, and RO) and technical expert teams (One ADB)
- Knowledge products and analytics

Work program and budget framework will reflect how differentiated approaches will be resourced.

DEVELOPING MEMBER COUNTRY

- FRA (contextual understanding on drivers of fragility and resilience factors)
- CPS partner in program development and COBP reflecting national priorities
- Country portfolio reviews and agreed action plans
- Adoption of digital technologies
- DMC performance monitoring

- Project implementation review and action plans reflecting context and changes
- Strategic FSA training and capacity development
- Strategic partnerships and coordination of national development programs

Facilitating FSA Implementation

SDCC Team
- Strategic technical support for FCAS from TA resource (for FRA and/or GRA work), analytics, knowledge products, and training courses (staff, DMCs)
- Interdepartmental coordination (OPs, private sector, STGs, RDs)
- FCAS classification
- Strategic partnerships (Working Groups, platforms with MDBs, CSOs, development partners)
- FSA Monitoring Framework including database and dashboard
- FSA Annual Report
- Watching briefs

SPD
- Operation manual, staff instructions and guidance notes (CPS, COBP)

PPFD
- Technical support on context-specific procedures

ADB = Asian Development Bank; COBP = country operations business plan; CPS= country partnership strategy; CSO = civil society organization; DMC = developing member country; FCAS = fragile and conflict-affected situations; FRA = fragility and resilience assessment; FSA = FCAS and SIDS Approach; GRA = governance risk assessment; ISGA = inclusive and sustainable growth assessment; MDB = multilateral development bank; OP = operational priority; PPFD = Procurement, Portfolio, and Financial Management Department; RD = regional department; RM = resident mission; RO = regional office; SDCC = Sustainable Development and Climate Change Department; SIDS = small island developing states; SPD = Strategy, Policy, and Partnerships Department; STG = sector and thematic group.

Source: ADB.

C. Strategic Partnerships and Coordination

ADB is a member of the Fragility Conflict and Violence Working Group with six other MDBs, which was established in October 2019.[48] Under this group, three technical sub-working groups were created in 2020 covering

(i) analytics with a focus on prevention, including risk and resilience assessments;
(ii) capacity building, learning, training, and knowledge exchange on fragility issues; and
(iii) results frameworks, and monitoring and evaluation in fragile settings. ADB contributes to these sub-working groups and fulfills rotational chairing duties in two of them.

ADB is a member of the MDB Platform on Forced Displacement and Economic Migration, established in 2017 with six other MDBs. The platform promotes cooperation and collaboration, in particular, on the intersection of FCAS and people on the move. ADB performs rotational chairing duties.

Partnerships with MDBs and development partners in global networks and platforms. ADB is a member of the International Network on Conflict and Fragility, which is a network of the OECD Development Assistance Committee members and key multilateral agencies working in fragile and conflict-affected contexts. The network promotes good practices and encourages learning from lessons, trends, and results delivery.

ADB is in discussions with the World Bank Global Crisis Risk Platform team, which is currently undertaking work on risk scanning, as part of an early warning system. The platform aims to foster strategic alignment among MDBs, strengthen operational collaboration, and promote knowledge sharing on issues of forcibly displaced people (e.g., refugees, returnees, and internally displaced persons), and economic migration. Through the platform, ADB engages on these subjects with organizations such as the Office of the UN High Commissioner for Refugees, International Organization for Migration, UN High-Level Panel on Internal Displacement, International Committee of the Red Cross, and the OECD.

ADB partnerships in subregional organizations. ADB's role as secretariat for subregional platforms (Central Asia Regional Economic Cooperation Program, Greater Mekong Subregion Program, South Asia Subregional Economic Cooperation Program) could involve preparing knowledge products and supporting consultations, to the extent feasible, on transboundary fragility and conflict-related issues. In the case of SIDS, discussing ways of efficiently addressing common vulnerabilities and conducting advocacy may best be carried out through subregional or regional platforms.

Leveraging knowledge and undertaking joint country-based analytical work. Opportunities are proactively being sought in FCAS and SIDS with other MDBs (World Bank, Islamic Development Bank) to undertake joint FRAs and other analytical work. A memorandum of understanding was signed with the UN Economic and Social Commission for Asia and the Pacific. Also, given its significant development programming role in the Pacific SIDS, ADB is seeking opportunities for analytics and knowledge sharing with development partners and organizations such as those in the Council of Regional Organisations of the Pacific, which have a long-term relationship with and understanding of the contextual environments of SIDS.

Expanded engagement with CSOs and other non-state organizations. A meaningful engagement will be undertaken in formal and informal contexts. Strengthening FCAS and SIDS engagement with ADB civil society forums, including women's groups, will involve in-country establishment of ADB–CSO consultative groups and platforms, including youth-led

---

[48] African Development Bank, European Bank for Reconstruction and Development, European Investment Bank, Inter-American Development Bank, Islamic Development Bank, and the World Bank.

engagement mechanisms. Active and inclusive CSO participation will take place during the development of FRAs and CPS preparation, and through consultation during project processing. This engagement is essential, especially in conflict contexts where state entities may not be able or willing to deliver services. A guidance note will be developed on frameworks to facilitate effective CSO engagement in FCAS and SIDS.

Country-based humanitarian–development–peace forums in conflict-affected DMCs, often led by the UN, are valuable consultative groups for further analysis, collaboration, and development of the country-specific interactions between humanitarian, development, and peacebuilding activities, and for joint approaches. Such forums also provide a mechanism for coordinated and complementary actions on gender inequality and violence, displacement and refugees, and other forms of social protection, as well as disaster risk and climate change management. While ADB's core focus is on supporting DMCs in their development agenda, this includes engaging in disaster and emergency assistance. There is a strong nexus between this type of development engagement and positive humanitarian impacts.

Working collaboratively in these forums will reinforce best practices and also support the FRA work in that it provides ADB with a strong analytical base to ensure that CPS programming

(i) reflects the impact of long-term conflict, climate change, or disasters on communities, especially on women and girls; and
(ii) takes into account humanitarian needs, social cohesion, loss of livelihood, displacement, and economic and political migration.

In undertaking ADB projects in FCAS and SIDS it will be essential to evaluate, through the FRA, the project's potential impacts on this humanitarian–development–peace nexus, to ensure that any negative impacts can be avoided or mitigated and that the project will build resilience.

D. Results Monitoring Framework and Reporting

To monitor performance in FCAS and SIDS, and to properly address issues as they arise will require a broader set of indicators than traditionally used. Currently used monitoring indicators may not fully reflect the country context or the effectiveness of project interventions in FCAS and SIDS environments, and the impact on evaluation at project completion. A broader set of indicators will be country- and context-specific based on the critical fragility and conflict assumptions (where relevant) that underlie risk-based programming and project interventions. Given that the context may be dynamic and the risk profiles changing, the indicator targets will need to offer flexibility to adapt and adjust to such changes.

In preparing projects in FCAS and SIDS contexts, at the design stage, the challenge lies in identifying those indicators that will enable monitoring

(i) how relevant and adaptive the interventions and their sequencing are, and
(ii) how effectively ADB engages with DMC clients, civil society, beneficiaries, and other stakeholders to achieve development objectives and outcomes.

In FCAS environments, and in those exposed to exogenous shocks, monitoring must involve both quantitative and qualitative indicators to enable a relevant measurement of development effectiveness, outcomes, and impacts.

It is anticipated that qualitative indicators may be used at country and project level to assess perception, achievement, and performance through surveys, reviews, and structured in-depth interviews with DMCs, beneficiaries, CSOs, implementing and development partners, and ADB and counterpart staff. The findings can be used to triangulate the effectiveness assessment.

In integrating identified fragility and conflict drivers and building on resilience factors in development interventions, it is essential that the multidimensional nature of the risks and their interlinks is understood. This is feasible with development interventions that are relatively straightforward, in that the links between the causal pathways and effects can be predicted and assessed. It is more challenging in complex development interventions where the multidimensional interlinkage of risks through numerous causal pathways and feedback loops compound over time; and often combined with exogenous events that results in limited clear delineation and predictability, and context-specific outcomes.

For complex interventions in FCAS and SIDS, while they may have sound designs with defined baselines, these will require greater flexibility and adaptiveness during implementation to respond in real time to context dynamics and unanticipated changes. Monitoring indicators (quantitative and qualitative) will be developed to incorporate responsiveness and flexibility during implementation.

At an operational level in FCAS and SIDS, the monitoring indicators will be embedded in the country program portfolio reviews, country development effectiveness reporting, and in project designs, and reported on during the regular project and portfolio performance reviews. In several FCAS and SIDS contexts, monitoring implementation performance is difficult because the projects are in geographical areas where operations face conflicts, remoteness, or low density of population and infrastructure. This is often compounded by limited counterpart data and related constraints.

To improve monitoring, ADB will build on existing efforts under ADB-supported project interventions to harness digital technology applications. It will work with FCAS DMCs and SIDS to increase uptake of and the capability for remote sensing and geospatial mapping and support the establishment of integrated digital databases. The digital technology outputs will be used to improve monitoring efficiency in FCAS and SIDS. Independent third-party monitoring will be undertaken where security and conflict risks and/or distance are an issue.

The FSA results framework is designed to assess the FSA implementation, performance, and effectiveness in facilitating institutional, behavioral, and procedural changes. The 18 results framework indicators include 13 existing ADB corporate results framework indicators[49] and five new indicators. Of the 13 existing indicators, three are FCAS- and SIDS-specific designed to look at ADB's organizational effectiveness and performance, and the results of its completed operations in FCAS and SIDS. Five new indicators are developed to capture ADB's results in using the differentiated approach, two of which are landmark FSA-defining indicators:

(i) applicable result areas from the seven OPs, disaggregated by FCAS and SIDS; and
(ii) operations that integrate differentiated approaches (contextualization, adaptiveness, responsiveness) throughout the project cycle.

These indicators will measure the institutionalization and outcome of the FSA from the design and implementation levels through to adaptive decision-making (exercising the differentiated approach in practice), and on to the achievement of development outcomes at DMC level. The progress on the FSA results framework will be reported to Management as part of the annual FSA report, and will complement the dedicated FCAS and SIDS chapters of the Development Effectiveness Review and Annual Portfolio Performance Report. The FSA results monitoring framework is outlined in Appendix 8.

In addition to the FSA indicators, an action tracker will monitor the FSA Action Plan implementation annually, with status updates provided for all ongoing sub-actions, including possible modifications. The action tracker will be added to a dedicated section of the FSA dashboard and details included in the annual FSA

---

[49] The ADB Corporate Results Framework consists of results framework indicators and tracking indicators.

report. In total, the FSA results framework proposes to monitor 18 indicators, 13 key action areas, and 34 sub-actions. The data will be collected through the existing ADB client and staff surveys and administrative data, disaggregated for FCAS and SIDS. Definitions and methodology (where necessary) of the indicators will be developed after the approval of the FSA.

The SDCC FCAS team is establishing an integrated database, using existing ADB data sources, to provide an analytic tool for monitoring and reporting on performance. This will also be used to assess and report on FSA progress and effectiveness. When required, the SDCC FCAS team will conduct strategic studies and assessments to provide further in-depth analysis and disseminate lessons to support departments that include FCAS and SIDS, and the FCAS network.

The SDCC FCAS team will prepare an annual FSA report for management on FSA achievements, adoption, and performance. A midterm review of the FSA will be undertaken in 2023, and an evaluation will be completed at completion of the FSA Action Plan implementation in 2025. The FSA report is a dedicated report on ADB's performance and achievements in FCAS DMCs and SIDS and it will expand the scope of reporting that is part of the annual Development Effectiveness Review and Portfolio Performance Report. The FSA report will be prepared every year before the annual ADF donors meeting.

Ensuring no one is left behind. Women's empowerment and education are key thrusts of Afghanistan's efforts to overcome fragility and conflict.

APPENDIX 1

FCAS and SIDS Approach Links with ADB Operational Priority Plans, and Sector and Thematic Areas

Strategy 2030 sets the course for the Asian Development Bank (ADB) to respond effectively to the region's changing needs. Under Strategy 2030, ADB will sustain its efforts to eradicate extreme poverty and expand its vision to achieve a prosperous, inclusive, resilient, and sustainable Asia and the Pacific. ADB's aspirations are aligned with major global commitments.[1]

Seven operational priorities (OPs) were defined to operationalize Strategy 2030, with operational plans developed for each priority to articulate the strategic focus, specific areas of engagement, approaches, and broad skills requirements. Each plan applies cross-sector and cross-thematic platforms and identifies differentiated approaches across fragile and conflict-affected situations (FCAS); small island developing states (SIDS); and lower, middle, and upper middle-income countries. In addition to the seven operational priority plans, ADB has an Operational Plan for Private Sector Operations, and thematic and sector plans. The plans prioritize ADB's support for the poorest and most vulnerable countries in the region, and for lagging areas and pockets of poverty and fragility across all country groups. They also help tailor ADB's business processes and strengthen its human resources and field presence in these countries.

As part of Strategy 2030, ADB is strengthening its country-focused approach using the country partnership strategy as the main platform to define customized support, promote the use of innovative technologies, and deliver integrated solutions by combining expertise across a range of sectors and themes and through a mix of public and private sector operations.

In developing a FCAS and SIDS approach (FSA) based on risk-informed decision-making methods in FCAS, SIDS, and pockets of poverty and fragility, it is essential to have a detailed understanding of the specific context, covering the causes, links, and multidimensional nature of the risks and resilience factors. Using an integrated approach to risk assessment, consistency is required across the operational priority, and thematic and sector plans when working in these contexts. The FSA will support Strategy 2030 in these contexts, and provide a consistent framework for analysis, as well as contextual knowledge that can be applied under One ADB approaches when preparing, processing, and implementing country programs and projects.

This appendix outlines ADB's planned support for FCAS and SIDS in each of the operational priority and private sector plans. The plans apply cross-sector and cross-thematic platforms that will harness and integrate expertise from (i) sector policies and working groups in education, energy, finance, health, transport, urban development, and water; and (ii) thematic groups in agriculture and food security, climate change and disaster risk management, environment, gender and development, safeguards governance and public management, information and communication technology, public–private partnerships, regional cooperation and integration, social development and poverty, and Sustainable Development Goals (SDGs).[2] These solutions will be delivered through innovative public and private sector operations appropriate to the specific needs in that FCAS and SIDS context.

Operational Plan for Priority 1 (OP1)—Addressing remaining poverty and reducing inequalities.[3] The plan addresses multidimensional poverty and supports the SDG agenda to tackle poverty and inequality and leave no one behind. It includes adopting differentiated approaches to FCAS; SIDS; and low-

---

[1] ADB. 2019. *Strategy 2030 Operational Plans Overview*. Manila.

[2] ADB sector and thematic areas.

[3] ADB. 2019. *Strategy 2030 Operational Plan for Priority 1: Addressing Remaining Poverty and Reducing Inequalities*. Manila.

income, lower middle-income, and upper middle-income countries. OP1 targets in particular the most vulnerable groups: women, indigenous peoples, ethnic minorities, persons with disabilities, hard-to-reach and remote populations, migrants, and internally displaced and/or conflict-affected people.

Operational Plan for Priority 2 (OP2)—Accelerating progress in gender equality.[4] The plan supports both SDG 5—to achieve gender equality and empower all women and girls—and the mainstreaming of gender-related targets and indicators across the other SDGs. Gender inequality is considered a driver of fragility and conflict and under pillar 5 of OP2, women's resilience to external shocks will be strengthened, and gender equality and women's empowerment measures will be integrated in post-conflict reconstruction operations, including supporting women's participation in the peacebuilding process, providing economic opportunities, and prioritizing basic infrastructure that meets the needs of women as well as measures to protect women from gender-based violence (SDG 16).

Operational Plan for Priority 3 (OP3)—Tackling climate change, building climate and disaster resilience, and enhancing environmental sustainability.[5] The plan promotes environmental sustainability in DMCs by addressing climate change, disaster risks, and environmental degradation; accelerating low greenhouse gas (GHG) emission development; ensuring a comprehensive approach to building climate and disaster resilience; and increasing the focus on the water–food–energy security nexus. OP3 is central to achieving 13 of the 17 SDGs. It has a core priority of increasing the quantity and quality of ADB investments toward mainstreaming climate change mitigation, climate and disaster resilience, and environmental sustainability; and integration across the water–food–energy security nexus, which is critical in FCAS and SIDS contexts.

Operational Plan for Priority 4 (OP4)—Making cities more livable.[6] The plan is to build livable, green, competitive, inclusive, and resilient cities and help DMCs develop the right institutions and policies. OP4 prioritizes support for the poorest and most vulnerable DMCs, including FCAS and SIDS. Targeting infrastructure deficits, environmental stress and degradation, climate change and disaster risk, social dimensions of migration, informal settlements, and aging societies, as well as governance and institutional capacity, it is well integrated with FCAS and SIDS contexts. OP4 support to cities in FCAS, in particular, will prioritize essential infrastructure and basic human needs, targeted social assistance, institutional strengthening of national and urban bodies, and governance reforms toward more functional urban environments. Activities in cities in FCAS will incorporate processes that promote peacebuilding, social cohesion, and cultural identity, recognizing the complex and fragile settings in their urban environments. Support to cities in SIDS will prioritize the strengthening of urban climate change and disaster resilience, promotion of environmental sustainability, and improvements in regional connectivity through internet access for business development and private sector participation.

Operational Plan for Priority 5 (OP5)—Promoting rural development and food security.[7] The objective is to improve market connectivity by transforming agricultural value-chain links. OP5 focuses on rural infrastructure and agri-logistics centers to enable the national, regional, and global integration of producers, agribusinesses, and consumers. It also aims to reduce postharvest losses and promotes agricultural value addition to increase rural incomes and enhance food security. OP5 supports the use of advanced technologies to increase productivity, ensure sustainable use of land and water resources, enhance food safety, and improve natural resource management. With a focused country approach to

---

[4] ADB. 2019. *Strategy 2030 Operational Plan for Priority 2: Accelerating Progress in Gender Equality.* Manila.

[5] ADB. 2019. *Strategy 2030 Operational Plan for Priority 3: Tackling Climate Change, Building Climate and Disaster Resilience, and Enhancing Environmental Sustainability.* Manila.

[6] ADB. 2019. *Strategy 2030 Operational Plan for Priority 4: Making Cities More Livable.* Manila.

[7] ADB. 2019. *Strategy 2030 Operational Plan for Priority 5: Promoting Rural Development and Food Security.* Manila.

ensure proper assessment and understanding of a DMC's specific situations, OP5 in FCAS countries will strengthen institutions, build policy dialogues, support reforms and capacity building, and include the introduction of smart technology for monitoring. In SIDS, OP5 helps strengthen disaster-coping mechanisms and meet non-climate-related needs for rural development and food security.

Operational Plan for Priority 6 (OP6)— Strengthening governance and institutional capacity.[8] The plan focuses on strengthening governance and institutional capacity and is aligned with SDGs 16 and 17. OP6 has the core focus of differentiated approaches in FCAS, SIDS, and DMCs that have subnational pockets of poverty, fragility, and conflict. ADB recognizes that better governance is not just a development outcome in itself, but serves as an enabler to achieve the other SDGs. Governance and sustainable development outcomes are intrinsically linked, and a country's governance, institutional capacity, and performance affect its achievement of the SDGs.

OP6 recognizes that there is no "one size fits all" approach, and the variability in governance and institutional capacity within and across DMCs demands differentiated policy and investment choices. OP6 requires approaches to be tailored to the unique context and circumstances of FCAS. They need to be informed by good diagnostics of a nation's political economy, the nature and causes of its fragility, and the roots of its conflict and then focus on strengthening state capacity and country systems to enable basic service delivery, improve legal and judicial systems, mitigate fraud and corruption, and bolster peace and stability. OP6 emphasizes the use of conflict-sensitive approaches for project identification and implementation, such as the fragility situation assessments and peacebuilding tools used in Afghanistan and the post-conflict transitional situation applied in Nepal.

Effective use of grant financing, including technical assistance (TA) grants, is a priority. Grant consideration needs to factor in a higher dependency on TA grants and greater need for advisory support across key ministries and institutions coupled with extended time horizons for translating outputs into outcomes. The use of policy-based lending will also contribute to setting a policy direction that complements institutional support. Likewise, OP6 recognizes the extreme vulnerabilities of SIDS, and calls for continued support of the use of flexible instruments to mobilize resources for disasters and climate change, and of greater private sector investments.

Operational Plan for Priority 7 (OP7)—Fostering regional cooperation and integration.[9] The plan supports regional cooperation and integration (RCI) by promoting market-driven regional integration and the production of regional public goods. Broadly, OP7 supports RCI operations in FCAS by contributing to infrastructure that economically links lagging border areas, including for special economic zones traversed by transnational transport corridors as part of ADB-supported subregional programs. It also promotes greater participation by small and medium-sized enterprises in local cross-border trade, and disaster risk mitigation and/or response mechanisms involving two or more DMCs. In the SIDS, OP7 supports the harmonization of policy among these states with global and regional agreements on trade, climate change adaptation, on-land and coastal and/or marine environmental sustainability and ocean health, and disaster risk management. Additionally, it considers strengthening cross-border connectivity, and sea and air transport, with information and communication technology (ICT) to enable small and medium-sized enterprises to take advantage of cross-border digital and merchandise trade. OP7 emphasizes institutional strengthening to support efforts to manage economic, climate change, and environmental and health risks; and to develop sustainable economic opportunities from shared natural resources, including healthy oceans.

---

[8] ADB. 2019. *Strategy 2030 Operational Plan for Priority 6: Strengthening Governance and Institutional Capacity.* Manila.
[9] ADB. 2019. *Strategy 2030 Operational Plan for Priority 7: Fostering Regional Cooperation and Integration.* Manila.

Operational Plan for Private Sector Operations.[10] The plan promotes the investment of private capital for development purposes, and aims to reduce remaining poverty and inequalities, and accelerate progress in gender equality, by supporting projects that generate quality jobs and livelihood opportunities, increase access to finance, and improve health and educational outcomes. The plan covers the sector, product, and special-initiative priorities of private sector operations (PSO), including in FCAS and SIDS. PSO will adapt existing products and champion new products and policies to increase and ensure ADB's competitiveness, market relevance, and leadership.

In FCAS, building on the foundations for private sector development led by sovereign operations, ADB will take a highly flexible approach to PSO. Support will likely focus on infrastructure with strong commercial viability and shorter-term paybacks—such as ICT and off-grid electricity—and on the improvement of banking systems and services, as well as funding for agriculture. ADB will also consider projects in areas that it would not typically support in larger or more mature markets—such as tourism, manufacturing, or services—as long as the projects are small individually and a minor part of the overall portfolio in aggregate. ADB will take on more risk when financing smaller businesses than it would undertake elsewhere, relying on portfolio diversification to manage risk and expedited policies to manage the flow of smaller transactions, as well as the considered use of concessional resources for blended finance and TA.

In SIDS, ADB is committed to engaging with the complex development issues, using an approach tailored to specific opportunities and challenges. It will invest in such areas as renewable energy; tourism; agribusiness, including fisheries; financial services; and ICT. As with FCAS, ADB will take a highly flexible approach and be willing to consider smaller and much higher-risk transactions with the considered use of blended finance and TA. Finally, incentives, including strong management support and performance measures, will be created for staff to increase the level of PSO in FCAS and SIDS.

---

[10] ADB. 2019. *Operational Plan for Private Sector Operations (2019–2024)*. Manila.

OP1 Addressing remaining poverty and reducing inequalities
- Human capital and social protection enhanced for all
- Quality jobs generated
- Access to opportunities increased for the most vulnerable

OP2 Accelerating progress in gender equality
- Women's economic empowerment increased
- Gender equality in human development enhanced
- Gender equality in decision-making and leadership enhanced
- Women's time poverty and drudgery reduced
- Women's resilience to external shocks strengthened

OP3 Tackling climate change, building climate and disaster resilience, and enhancing environmental sustainability
- Mitigation of climate change increased
- Climate and disaster resilience built
- Environmental sustainability enhaced

OP4 Making cities more livable
- Improve access, quality and reliability of services in urban areas
- Strengthen urban planning and financial sustainability of cities
- Improve urban environment, climate-resilience, and disaster management of cities
- Women's time poverty and drudgery reduced
- Women's resilience to external shocks strengthened

OP5 Promoting rural development and food security
- Rural development
- Agricultural value chains
- Food security

OP6 Strengthening governance and institutional capacity
- Strengthened public management and financial stability
- Enhanced governance and institutional capacity for service delivery
- Strengthened country systems and standards

OP7 Fostering regional cooperation and integration
- Greater and higher quality connectivity between economies
- Global and regional trade and investment opportunities expanded
- Regional public goods increased and diversified

Operational Plan for Private Sector Operations
- Supporting quality jobs and livelihood opportunities
- Increase access to finance
- Improve health and educational outcomes

APPENDIX 2
Evolution of ADB's FCAS Agenda

2004
Approach to Weakly-Performing Development Member Countries - A discussion paper

2005 — Paris Declaration on Aid Effectiveness

2007 — The Principle for Good International Engagement in Fragile States and Situations
Achieving Development Effectiveness in Weakly - Performing Countries

2008 — Accra Agenda for Action
Strategy 2020

2010
Asian Development Bank's Support to Fragile and Conflict-Affected Situations Special Evaluation Study - IED

2011 — Busan New Deal for Engagement in Fragile States

Working Differently in Fragile and Conflict-Affected Situations

2012

2013

Operational Plan for Enhancing ADB's Effectiveness in FCAS

2014

Mapping Fragile and Conflict-Affected Situations in Asia and the Pacific: The ADB Experience

2021

FCAS and SIDS Approach

2019
Relevance and Results of Concessional Finance: Asian Development Fund XI and 12 Corporate Evaluation Study - IED

2018
Strategy 2030

2016
2016-2020 Fragility Sensitivity Approach to the Pacific

Sustainable Development Goals (SDGs)

2015
Asian Development Fund X and XI Operations Corporate Evaluation Study - IED

ADB = Asian Development Bank, FCAS = fragile and conflict-affected situations, IED = Independent Evaluation Department, SIDS = small island development state.
Source: Asian Development Bank.

APPENDIX 3
Asian Development Fund Grant and Concessional Ordinary Capital Resources Lending

Grants are needed in Asia and the Pacific to support developing member countries (DMCs) facing high or moderate risk of debt distress[1] and to support debt sustainability by avoiding the increase of debt burdens on countries. The need for grant support has further increased since the coronavirus disease (COVID-19) pandemic exacerbated countries' debt vulnerabilities. Grants can also play a catalytic role to support investments in targeted areas such as gender equality; climate adaptation and disaster risk reduction; and regional public goods (RPGs), including regional health security.

The DMCs of the Asian Development Bank (ADB) that are eligible for Asian Development Fund (ADF) grants and concessional ordinary capital resources lending (COL) are group A and group B countries, also called the concessional assistance countries.[2] Group A countries are further differentiated to determine the mix of ADF and COL they can access, based on ADB's concessional assistance policy for the ADF 13 period.[3] Following the combination of ADF lending operations with the ordinary capital resources (OCR) balance sheet, which took effect on 1 January 2017, the ADF has become a grant-only fund while COL is funded from ADB's OCR balance sheet.[4]

Donors agreed during the ADF 13 negotiations on a total replenishment of $4,061 million for the period 2021–2024,[5] which includes an allocation of $3,198 million for ADF grant financing and an allocation of $517 million for the Technical Assistance Special Fund (TASF) 7.[6]

ADF 13 will be the first ADF cycle to support the implementation of ADB's corporate strategy—Strategy 2030—during its full cycle and will fund key agendas in eligible countries, which include a majority of DMCs classified as fragile and conflict-affected situations (FCAS), such as Afghanistan, and the small island developing states (SIDS). The ADF 13 resource allocation framework adopts a two-pillar approach with country- and theme-based components. The performance-based allocation system remains the cornerstone of the ADF 13 grant allocation framework. The single thematic pool encourages governments to consider projects with significant content of regional cooperation and integration (RCI); RPGs, including regional health security, disaster risk reduction, and climate change adaptation; and the transformative gender agenda of Sustainable Development Goal (SDG) 5. The ADF grant reserve for changes in debt distress is intended to finance growing demand for ADF grants because of the deteriorating situation in eligible countries when it comes to the risk of debt distress (footnote 3).

Other areas of special attention under ADF 13 include quality infrastructure in line with the principles of the Group of 20, strong governance, development of private sector operations, and debt sustainability through the implementation of the Sustainable Development Finance Policy, in close coordination

---

[1] Debt distress classification is based on the joint International Monetary Fund–World Bank Debt Sustainability Framework for low-income countries for debt-sustainability analyses.

[2] ADB uses a three-tier DMC classification system: groups A, B, and C. Classification is determined by two criteria: gross national income per capita (Atlas method) and creditworthiness. Group A countries are DMCs lacking creditworthiness. Group B countries are those with limited creditworthiness. Group C countries have adequate creditworthiness and per capita incomes exceeding the operational cut-off of the World Bank's International Development Association. Access to ADF grants and COL for group A countries is determined by the risk of debt distress. ADF grants are also provided to support specific challenges. Group B countries have access to COL and regular OCR lending. Group C countries have access to regular OCR lending.

[3] ADB. 2020. *Concessional Assistance Policy for the ADF 13 Period*. Manila.

[4] ADB. 2015. *Enhancing ADB's Financial Capacity for Reducing Poverty in Asia and the Pacific*. Manila.

[5] ADB. 2020. *ADF 13 Donors' Report: Tackling the Covid-19 Pandemic and Building a Sustainable and Inclusive Recovery in Line with Strategy 2030*. Manila.

[6] The ADF 13 financing requirements also include an amount of $346 million for administrative expenses.

Table A3.1: 2021 Classification of Developing Member Countries Asian Development Fund 13

Group A: Concessional Assistance-only (CA-only)				Group B: OCR Blend (COL and regular OCR)
ADF-eligible[a]			COL-only Gap[b]	
ADF-only (100% grant)	ADF Blend (50% grant)	COL-only (0% grant)		
Afghanistan*f Federated States of Micronesia f Kiribati*fσ Marshall Islands fσ Maldives σ Nauru fσ Samoa σ Tajikistan Tonga σ Tuvalu*fσ	Kyrgyz Republic Solomon Islands*fσ Vanuatu σ	Nepal*	Bhutan* Cambodia* Lao PDR*f Myanmar*f	Bangladesh* Mongolia Pakistan Palau σ Papua New Guinea f Timor-Leste*fσ Uzbekistan

* = least developed, *f* = fragile and conflict-affected situations, σ = small island developing states, ADF = Asian Development Fund, COL = Concessional OCR lending, Lao PDR = Lao People's Democratic Republic, OCR = ordinary capital resources.

[a] ADF eligibility refers to eligibility for country allocations.
[b] Gap countries are designated as such by the International Development Association and are ineligible for ADF grant country allocation under ADB's concessional assistance policy.

Source: ADB. https://www.adb.org/what-we-do/public-sector-financing/lending-policies-rates.

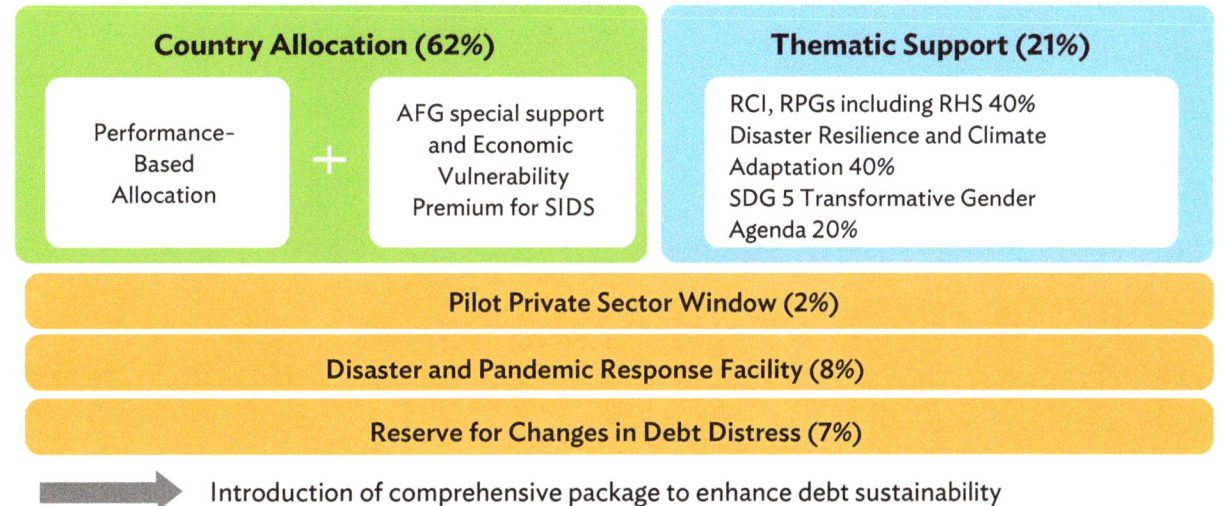

Figure A3: Asian Development Fund 13 Grant Allocation Framework

AFG = Afghanistan, RCI = regional cooperation and integration, RHS= regional health security, RPGs = regional public goods, SDG = Sustainable Development Goal, SIDS = small island developing states.
Source: Asian Development Bank.

with the Word Bank's International Development Association and the International Monetary Fund, which will also improve debt transparency. All areas of special attention support the response to the COVID-19 pandemic and help build the foundations of an inclusive and sustainable economic recovery in ADF and COL countries. Figure A.3 shows the ADF grant allocation framework.

TASF 7 will continue to support capacity building, policy advice, and knowledge production and will have an increased focus on strengthening debt sustainability in ADF and COL countries.

Components of the Asian Development Fund 13 Framework Relevant for FCAS and SIDS

Special allocation for Afghanistan. Despite important results of ADB operations in energy, transport, and agriculture and natural resources, Afghanistan continues to be classified as an FCAS and has extensive development needs. Continued efforts and investments are needed to tackle the country's remaining social and economic challenges.[7]

Economic vulnerability premium for SIDS. A premium calibrated based on the economic vulnerability index will complement performance-based allocations for ADF-eligible SIDS. Based on their index scores, ADF-eligible SIDS are assigned premium amounts.

Single thematic pool. The thematic pool provides ADF grants to encourage governments to consider projects with strong national and regional positive externalities and to support the implementation of Strategy 2030 with a focus on the following strategic areas: (i) fostering RCI, including the provision of RPGs; (ii) supporting disaster risk reduction and climate adaptation; and (iii) achieving SDG 5's transformative gender agenda. Regional health security will be supported along with RCI and RPGs. Priority access is given to FCAS and SIDS.

Piloting the private sector window. ADF 13 introduces on a pilot basis a private sector window (PSW). The PSW will contribute to reducing some of the shared financing constraints that hinder private sector operations in group A countries. The need to de-risk private sector investments was very strong before COVID-19, and that need has increased as businesses try to access financing to kick-start and rebuild operations that were adversely impacted by the pandemic. The PSW includes three solutions: local currency loans, blended finance, and loan guarantees. It does not provide indicative allocations among the three solutions. The allocation of resources will be flexible, with no ceilings on country, sector, or other limits for any of the solutions proposed. While it is critical that the PSW retains optimal flexibility to respond to the emerging needs of group A countries, ADB will ensure that the PSW maintains a balance across countries, sectors, and products to deploy resources across eligible group A countries for transactions that meet the PSW eligibility criteria.

Enhancing debt sustainability. Support for debt sustainability in ADF and COL countries will be strengthened by aligning it with the Sustainable Development Finance Policy principles of International Development Association.

Expanded disaster and pandemic response facility. The expanded Disaster and Pandemic Response Facility (DRF+) provides assistance to eligible countries through a more predictable financing source to cover the costs of disaster and emergency assistance, early recovery, and reconstruction after a disaster. DRF+ covers disasters triggered by natural hazards, large cross-border movements of displaced persons, and public health emergencies such as epidemics and pandemics.

TASF 7. The TASF plays a critical role in implementing Strategy 2030 as the primary instrument for supporting DMCs in (i) project preparation and implementation, (ii) capacity building, and (iii) knowledge generation and innovation. TA for group A and B countries will focus on debt sustainability, capacity building in project preparation and implementation, the handling of vulnerabilities, and policy reforms.[8] Table A3.2 provides indicative ADF 13 allocations.[9]

---

[7] ADB. 2020. *Afghanistan: Progress and Remaining Challenges (Supplementary Note)*. Paper prepared for the second ADF 13 replenishment meeting. Philippines. 11–12 February.

[8] ADB. 2019. *Seventh Replenishment of the Technical Assistance Special Fund*. Manila.

[9] The overall grant amount agreed with ADF donors of $3,198 million was subsequently increased to $3,328 million to include a carryover resource from ADF 12.

Table A3.2: Asian Development Fund 13 Indicative Allocations

Item	Amount ($ million)
Country allocation	2,064
Of which: Performance-based allocation	1,165
Special support to Afghanistan	486
SIDS premium	413
Thematic pool	699
Pilot of Private Sector Window	67
Enhanced Disaster and Pandemic Response Facility	266
Reserve for changes in debt distress	233
Total ADF Grants	**3,328**
Memorandum items:	
FCAS	**1,245**
SIDS	**576**

ADF = Asian Development Fund, FCAS = fragile and conflict-affected situations, SIDS = small island developing states.

Note: Numbers may not sum precisely because of rounding.

Source: Asian Development Bank.

APPENDIX 4
Problem Analysis

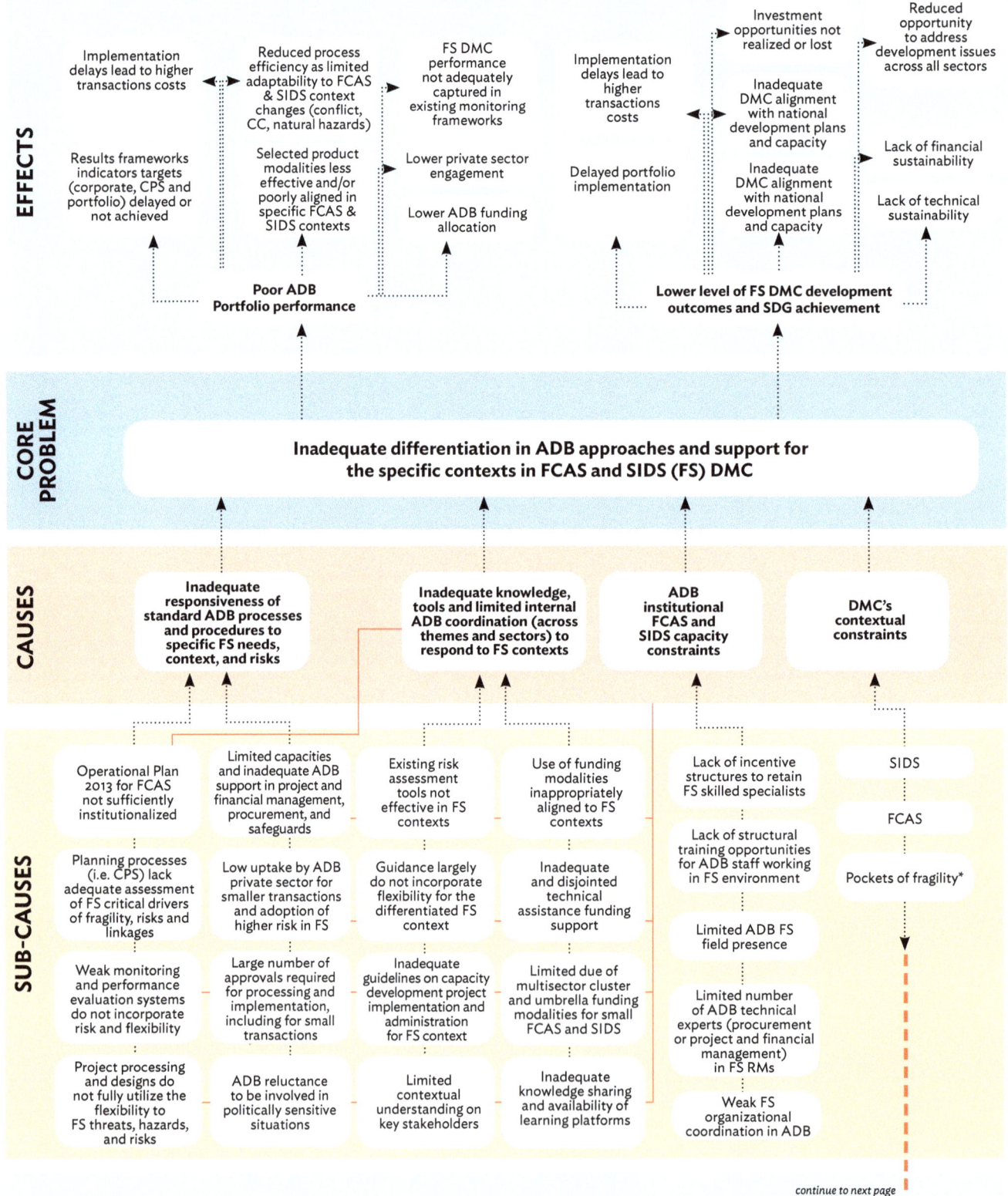

ADB = Asian Development Bank, CPS = country partnership strategy, CSO = civil society organization, DMC = developing member country, FCAS = fragile and conflict-affected situations, FS = FCAS and SIDS, RM = resident mission, SDG = Sustainable Development Goal, SIDS = small island developing states.

Source: Asian Development Bank.

Appendix 4

continued from previous page

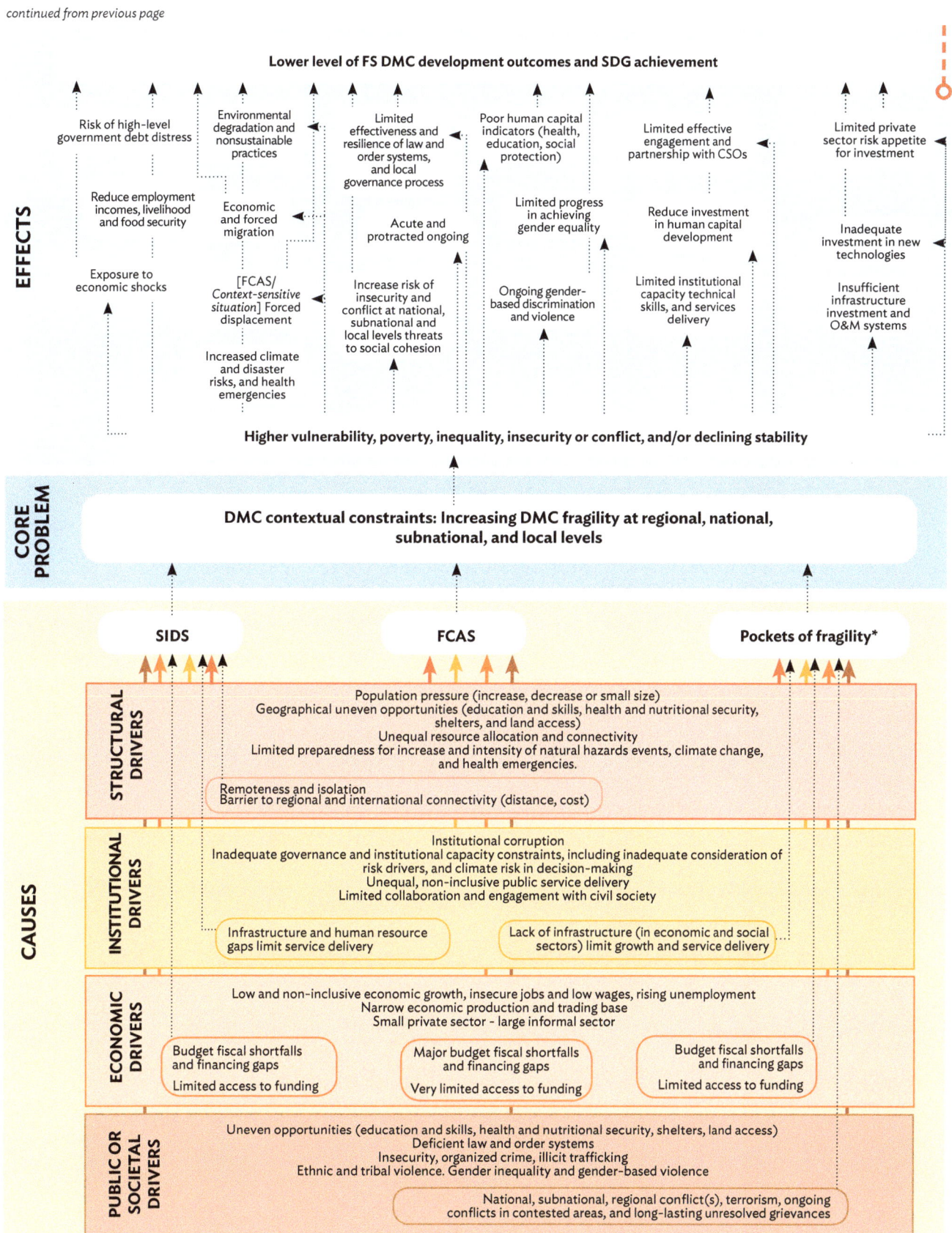

* Areas in non-designated FCAS DMCs, including in upper-middle-income countries that experience persistent poverty caused by fragility and/or conflict, as defined in Strategy 2030. 2018. ADB Strategy 2030. Manila. p. 13, para. 30.

ADB = Asian Development Bank, CSO = civil society organization, DMC = developing member country, FCAS = fragile and conflict-affected situations, FS = FCAS and SIDS, O&M = operation and maintenance, SDG = Sustainable Development Goal, SIDS = small island developing states.

Source: Asian Development Bank.

APPENDIX 5
Theory of Change and Links to Corporate Results

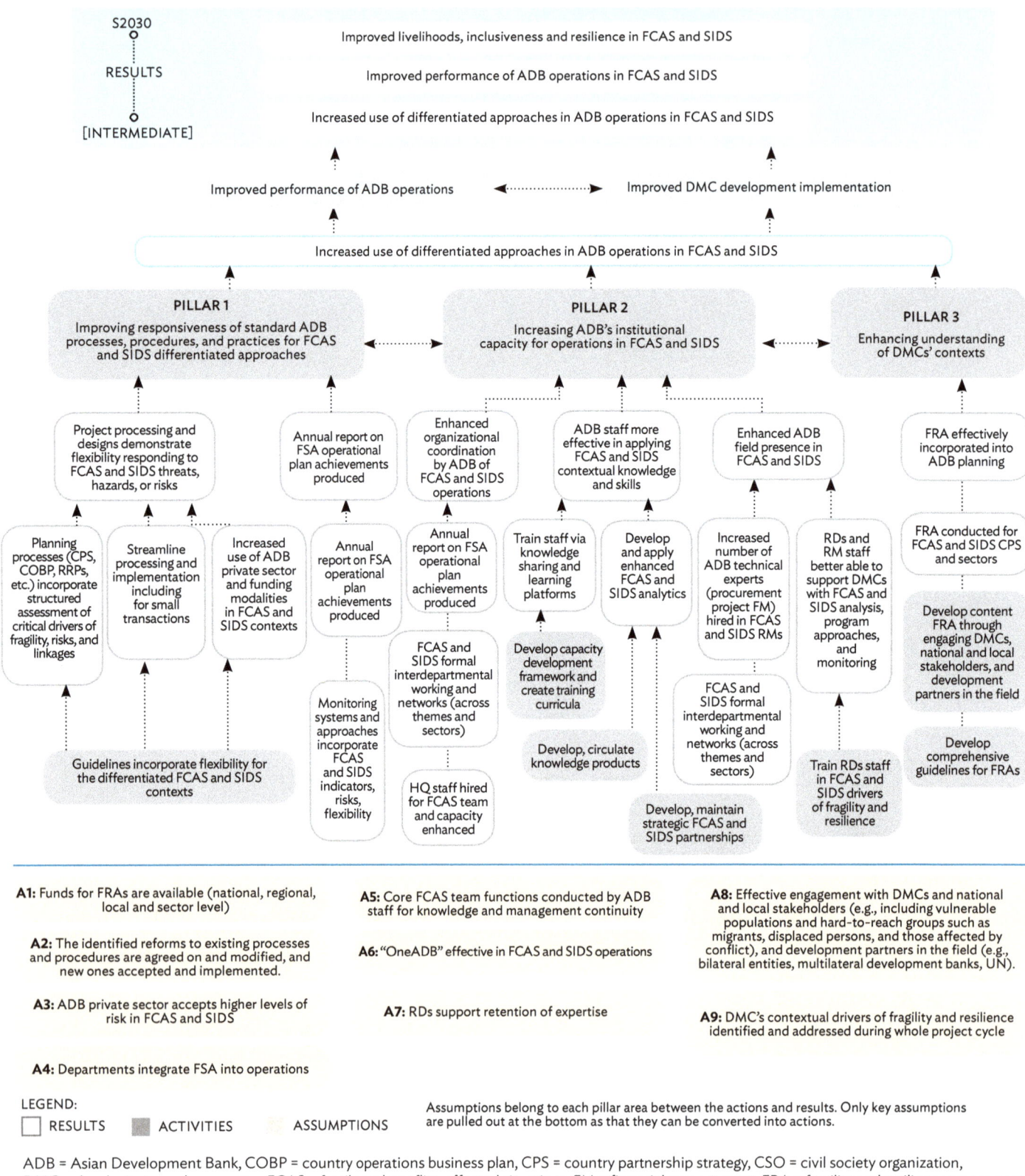

ADB = Asian Development Bank, COBP = country operations business plan, CPS = country partnership strategy, CSO = civil society organization, DMC = developing member country, FCAS = fragile and conflict-affected situations, FM = financial management, FRA = fragility and resilience assessment, FS = FCAS and SIDS, HQ = headquarters, MDB = multilateral development bank, O&M = operation and maintenance, RD = regional department, RM = resident mission, RRP = report and recommendation of the President, S2030 = Strategy 2030, SDG = Sustainable Development Goal, SIDS = small island developing states, UN = United Nations.

Source: Asian Development Bank.

The theory of change (TOC) guiding the fragile and conflict-affected situations (FCAS) and small island developing states (SIDS) approach (FSA) is derived from the problem analysis and the identified root causes (Appendix 4). The TOC is an analytical approach for undertaking solution development and results analysis, which are two iterative processes that inform each other[1] by converting problems into solutions and arranging them in causal pathways where each action area result is preceded by its necessary precondition(s). The TOC diagram illustrates step by step the process required to achieve the three outcomes. The model makes critical assumptions explicit so that they can be routinely revisited while implementing an intervention. If these assumptions do not hold true, they become barriers to the full implementation of the intervention, and require the introduction of corrective actions by the implementing bodies.

The TOC identifies what changes are required to achieve higher levels of development outcomes, improved implementation by developing member countries (DMCs), and improved performance of Asian Development Bank (ADB) operations in FCAS, SIDS, and other context-sensitive areas. The TOC defines, as underlying activities, the differentiation of ADB's approaches through three pillars, each with its own outcome—pillar 1: improving responsiveness of standard ADB processes, procedures, and practices for FCAS and SIDS differentiated approaches; pillar 2: increasing ADB's institutional capacity for FCAS and SIDS contexts; and pillar 3: improving ADB's contextual analysis and understanding of DMCs.

Pillar 1: Improving Responsiveness of Standard ADB Processes, Procedures, and Practices for FCAS and SIDS Differentiated Approaches

This outcome is achieved through a series of activities and results linked to one another through causality. Starting from the first actions at the bottom of the pathway, the FSA is drafted by (i) analyzing the previous FCAS operational plan (2013) and deriving lessons; (ii) conducting stakeholder consultations in ADB's operational and support departments, and with development partners; and (iii) examining ADB's internal processes and procedures and identifying those that will need to be adapted or need to accommodate additional flexibility to implement the FSA. Once approved, the FSA will serve as a road map—through the action plan and related action tracker—for introducing and carrying forward, across the designated departments, appropriate changes in the identified business processes and procedures (Appendix 7). Contextual analyses of DMCs (that identify the critical drivers of fragility and their interlinks with conflict (where appropriate) (pillar 3) and the risks to ADB operations will then provide the basis for tailored responses that will be incorporated into project planning, design, and implementation as well as in country partnership strategies (CPSs) and country operations business plans.

---

[1] ADB. 2020. *Guidelines for preparing and using a design and monitoring framework.* Manila.

These actions and results—monitored using the accompanying indicator—are based on the assumptions that:

- Funds to support project contextualised readiness will be available (assumption A1):

Assumption	Indicator
A1: Funds are available for fragility and resilience assessments (national, regional, local, and sector level).	Action tracker: Level of congruence between fragility assessment funding needs and disbursements.

- Business processes and procedures are adapted to include the necessary flexibility in FCAS and SIDS (assumption A2):

Assumption	Indicator
A2: The identified reforms to existing processes and procedures are agreed on and modified, and new ones accepted and implemented.	Action tracker: Endorsement of identified business process and procedures changes.

- Increased engagement of private sector financing in FCAS and SIDS with ADB accepting higher risk levels (assumption A3):

Assumption	Indicator
A3: ADB private sector financing accepts higher levels of risk in FCAS and SIDS.	Number and $ value of ADB private sector loans. Completed operations rated successful (%, nonsovereign operations): a. Development results, b. ADB's additionality, c. ADB's work quality (corporate results framework–tracking indicator).

With the preparatory work completed in this pillar, project processing and designs will include the flexibility required for operations in FCAS and SIDS. This level of achievement is predicated on the departments integrating FSA into their operations, as captured in assumption A4:

Assumption	Indicator
A4: Departments integrate FSA into operations.	CPS integrating differentiated approaches (New). Projects integrating differentiated approaches in the project cycle (%) (New). Staff reporting improved knowledge, understanding, and use of the differentiated approaches (%) (New).

The second causal pathway in pillar 1 focuses on monitoring and measurement. To ensure the adequacy of the FSA's responsiveness, it will be necessary to monitor, measure, and analyze data, and if necessary, adapt during implementation. This pathway begins with defining the monitoring framework to incorporate FCAS and SIDS indicators, risks, and flexibility. At the same time, there is emphasis on building the capacity of the Sustainable Development and Climate Change Department (SDCC) FCAS team members for measuring performance so as to provide appropriate levels of monitoring and reporting to support the FSA implementation in ADB. This will allow for the creation of a dashboard to store and retrieve the required data. It will also provide the foundation for the creation of evidence-based reporting on the state of the FSA.

Pillar 2: Increasing ADB's Institutional Capacity for Operations in FCAS and SIDS

The first pathway under pillar 2 addresses a functional need of the SDCC FCAS team. It begins with defining the SDCC FCAS team structure, including the human resources plan with terms of reference for new staff positions. The plan is then funded with adequate and recurrent budget fort staff who take on core FCAS functions. To ensure institutional continuity, an assumption is that core SDCC FCAS team functions will be conducted by permanent staff:

Assumption	Indicator
A5: Core FCAS team functions conducted by ADB staff for knowledge and management continuity.	Action tracker: Terms of reference and recruitment process.

With the addition of new skilled staff, the SDCC FCAS team will be positioned to support interdepartmental working and network development. An assumption made is that ADB will function as One ADB in its approach to integrating the FSA into its operations:

Assumption	Indicator
A6: One ADB effective in FCAS and SIDS operations.	Not applicable.

The next pathway in pillar 2 focuses on knowledge and skills development. It begins with activities that develop guidelines based on a training needs analysis in the FCAS and SIDS context. From these guidelines, FSA training modules, knowledge sharing, and learning platforms are created and training is delivered to appropriate ADB staff and DMC counterparts. At the same time, FCAS and SIDS analytics, knowledge products, and tools are developed or updated. In parallel, strategic relationships are broadened or reinforced with development partners. Implemented successfully, this work will enhance staff effectiveness in applying contextual knowledge and skills.

The final pathway under pillar 2 enhances ADB's field presence in FCAS and SIDS by training the existing complement of staff or by repurposing the vacant positions, and by hiring consultants. Activities focus on enforcing or adapting human resources budgets and policies to promote an effective incentive structure. This work enables to strengthen ADB's field presence.

Assumption	Indicator
A7: Regional departments support retention of expertise.	Budgeted international and national staff positions in FCAS and SIDS field offices. Operations administered in field offices (%, sovereign). Filled international and national staff positions in FCAS and SIDS resident missions and field offices (number).

Concurrently, training will be implemented to support targeted staff in the identification and "use" of drivers of fragility and resilience so as to support DMCs with adapted program design, implementation, and monitoring.

Pillar 3: Enhancing Understanding of DMC Contexts

Pillar 3 focuses on enhancing the institutional understanding of FCAS, SIDS, and other pockets of fragility, primarily through the effective use of fragility and resilience assessments (FRAs) in the planning processes. The work begins with ADB developing guidelines on preparing FRAs. The guidelines will provide for the inclusion of several consultations. The assumption that is made is that the consultations will occur with the necessary target groups and not only in number, but also in quality.

Assumption	Indicator
A8: Effective engagement with DMCs and national and local stakeholders (e.g., including vulnerable populations and hard to reach groups such as migrants, displaced persons, and those affected by conflict), and development partners in the field (e.g., bilateral entities, multilateral development banks, United Nations).	Not applicable.

Once FRAs have been conducted, they need to be fully understood and owned by ADB's resident missions, field offices, and DMCs. An important assumption is that the critical issues, analysis, and findings raised in the FRAs will be thoroughly considered and integrated into CPSs and project plans:

Assumption	Indicator
A9: DMC's contextual drivers of fragility and resilience identified and addressed during whole project cycle.	Action tracker: FRA and consultation staff instructions and guidelines (as appropriate) developed.

APPENDIX 6
FCAS and SIDS Approach Action Plan 2021–2025

New | ● Continuous activity with deliverables | ● Discrete activity with deliverables | ● Deliverables

PILLAR 1 — Improving Responsiveness of Standard ADB Processes, Procedures, and Practices for FCAS and SIDS Differentiated Approaches

KEY ACTION AREA 1
Adoption of risk based strategic and business processes

KAA 1 — sub-action 1 (New)
Integrate the FRA in the diagnostic work for CPS preparation, in the CPS programming and the COBP. Monitor context changes (as part of CPS monitoring) and revise programming as required.
LEAD RDs SUPPORT SDCC

KAA 1 — sub-action 2 (New)
Introduce new/revamped business processes, procedures and guidelines that incorporate flexibility for FCAS and SIDS. (Refer to Appendix 7 for details on priority business processes and procedures reforms).
LEAD SPD and SDCC/PPFD SUPPORT RDs

KAA 1 — sub-action 3
Streamline business processes for small nonsovereign transactions.
LEAD PSOD SUPPORT ORM, SPD, OGC, RDs

KAA 1 — sub-action 4
Provide technical support to clarify and improve use and adoption of flexibilities under existing business processes and procedures.
LEAD SDCC, PPFD SUPPORT RDs

KEY ACTION AREA 2
FCAS and SIDS responsive project modalities in operational use

KAA 2 — sub-action 1
Increase use of diversified products, instruments and funding modalities (including under ADF 13) and blended financing.
LEAD RDs, PSOD SUPPORT SDCC

KAA 2 — sub-action 2
Increase uptake of smaller nonsovereign transactions.
LEAD SDCC SUPPORT PPFD, SPD, RDs

KEY ACTION AREA 3
Context appropriate project preparation, design and implementation procedures

KAA 3 — sub-action 1 (New)
Integrating FRA findings and resilience actions for the specific locational context in project preparation and design. For conflict affected DMCs, security risk assessment with regular updating is mandatory.
LEAD RDs SUPPORT PSOD, SDCC, OAS

KAA 3 — sub-action 2
Increase in the use of project readiness financing and small expenditure financing facilities to enhance project readiness, especially for larger infrastructure projects.
LEAD RDs SUPPORT PSOD, SPD, SDCC

KAA 3 — sub-action 3
Increase the use of alternative and innovative project design and implementation arrangements with enhanced project preparation.
LEAD RDs SUPPORT PSOD, SDCC, OAG

KAA 3 — sub-action 4
Undertake capacity assessments of executing and implementing agency and prepare support plan that is incorporated into project design and related documents.
LEAD RDs SUPPORT PSOD, SDCC

KEY ACTION AREA 4
Integration of digital technologies

KAA 4 — sub-action 1
Support the development and integration of digital technologies appropriate for FCAS and SIDS contexts (for preparation, implementation, and monitoring) and establishment of integrated digital databases.
LEAD RDs SUPPORT SDCC, SPD

KEY ACTION AREA 5
FCAS and SIDS responsive monitoring and reporting systems operational

KAA 5 — sub-action 1 (New)
Develop the methodology and the performance standards in FSA result framework.
LEAD SDCC SUPPORT SPD, RDs

KAA 5 — sub-action 2 (New)
Develop and maintain a dedicated FCAS and SIDS dashboard.
LEAD SDCC SUPPORT PPFD, SPD, RDs

KAA 5 — sub-action 3 (New)
Report annually to management on FSA achievements and performance of FCAS and SIDS as per ADF commitments.
LEAD SDCC SUPPORT SPD, RDs

Timeline

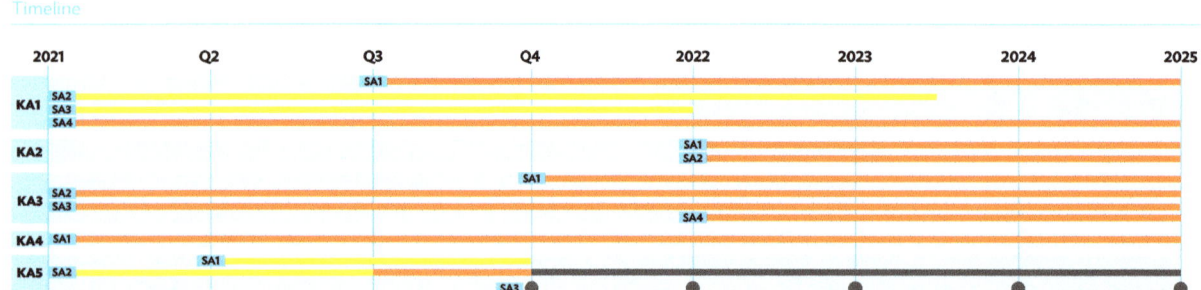

ADB = Asian Development Bank; ADF = Asian Development Fund; COBP = country operations business plan; CPS = country partnership strategy; FCAS = fragile and conflict-affected situations; FRA = fragility and resilience assessment; FSA = FCAS and SIDS Approach; KAA = key action area; OAG = Office of the Auditor General; OAS = Office of Administrative Services; OGC = Office of the General Counsel; ORM = Office of Risk Management; PPFD = Procurement, Portfolio, and Financial Management Department; PSOD = Private Sector Operations Department; Q = quarter; RD = regional department; SA = sub-action; SDCC = Sustainable Development and Climate Change Department; SIDS = small island developing states; SPD = Strategy, Policy, and Partnerships Department.

Source: Asian Development Bank.

● New ● Continuous activity with deliverables ● Discrete activity with deliverables ● Deliverables

PILLAR 2 — Increasing ADB's Institutional Capacity for Operations in FCAS and SIDS

KEY ACTION AREA 1
Enhanced ADB FCAS and SIDS organizational coordination

KAA 1 — sub-action 1
Provide adequate staff (with the required mix of skills and expertise) and resources for the FCAS team to undertake FSA functions, including application of the FCAS lens in key areas of operations (themes and sectors).
LEAD SDCC SUPPORT BPMSD

KAA 1 — sub-action 2
Formalize and operate FCAS and SIDS working groups and networks across themes and sectors.
LEAD SDCC SUPPORT All departments

KAA 1 — sub-action 3
Support the FCAS anchors across regional departments, resident missions, sectors, and thematic groups. This will include FCAS team advisory support, participating in sector and country teams, and providing TA resources.
LEAD SDCC SUPPORT RDs

KAA 1 — sub-action 4
Extend existing or prepare new technical assistance projects for DMCs to ensure adequate and consistent support to FCAS and SIDS operations. This to include innovative use of technologies and training based on DMCs training needs analysis.
LEAD SDCC SUPPORT SPD

KAA 1 — sub-action 5
Develop and implement the FSA communications strategy, plan, and tools to promote and facilitate knowledge sharing and cultural change.
LEAD SDCC SUPPORT DOC

KEY ACTION AREA 2
Strengthened knowledge and analytics

KAA 2 — sub-action 1
Develop data analytics and tools to support analysis of geographically specific fragility, poverty, conflict, and other parameters, including classifications.
LEAD SDCC SUPPORT ERCD

KAA 2 — sub-action 2
Strengthening analytics and knowledge products based on the analytics needs assessment, and enhance knowledge management and transfer utilizing ADB knowledge networks.
LEAD SDCC SUPPORT RDs

KEY ACTION AREA 3
ADB staff more effective in applying FCAS and SIDS contextual knowledge and skills

KAA 3 — sub-action 1
Develop a competency framework, prepare FCAS and SIDS training content based on the training need analysis, and support a peer mentoring program.
LEAD SDCC SUPPORT RDs

KAA 3 — sub-action 2
Develop and deliver specific training modules to staff assigned in FCAS and SIDS (ADF 13 commitment) and in ADB induction program basic training modules.
LEAD SDCC SUPPORT BPMSD

KAA 3 — sub-action 3
Training ADB staff in institutional capacity development approaches for FCAS and SIDS contexts to support government functions and sustain the transition toward resilience.
LEAD SDCC SUPPORT BPMSD

KEY ACTION AREA 4
Enhanced ADB responsiveness

KAA 4 — sub-action 1
Strengthen field presence (RMs and ROs) and harness and pool cross-regional expertise (sector, thematic, implementation, procurement, financial management and safeguards).
LEAD RDs, BPMSD SUPPORT SDCC

KAA 4 — sub-action 2
Develop contextual terms of reference to attract experienced and motivated staff and/or consultants and apply specific recruitment strategies for FCAS and SIDS-experienced international and national consultants.
LEAD RDs SUPPORT BPMSD, PPFD, SDCC

KEY ACTION AREA 5
Stronger human resource policies and enhanced incentives

KAA 5 — sub-action 1
Effective incentive (financial and non-financial) structures applied to attract and retain skilled staff in FCAS and SIDS. Raise awareness on the incentive schemes and promote mobilization of competent and motivated staff.
LEAD BPMSD SUPPORT RDs

KAA 5 — sub-action 2
Incentivize and encourage further uptake of short-term assignment (STA) for FCAS and SIDS national staff to promote exposure and awareness among sectors and regions and develop a talent pool.
LEAD RDs SUPPORT BPMSD

KEY ACTION AREA 6
Expanded partnerships and coordination

KAA 6 — sub-action 1
Expand partnerships and engagement at the global, regional, and country level for analytic and knowledge sharing, training, capacity building, and joint assessment work in DMCs.
LEAD SDCC SUPPORT RDs, SPD

KAA 6 — sub-action 2
Increased coordination at country level with DMCs and development partners on joint programming, funding, and cofinancing opportunities. In conflict DMCs participate in humanitarian development peace-building forums.
LEAD RDs SUPPORT SDCC

Timeline

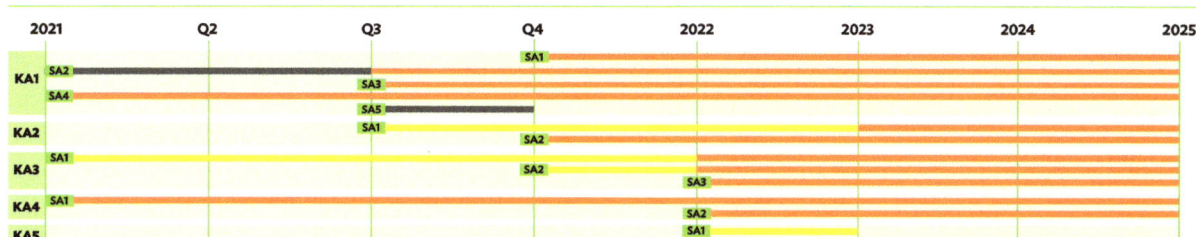

ADB = Asian Development Bank; ADF = Asian Development Fund; BPMSD = Budget, People, and Management Systems Department; COBP = country operations business plan; CPS = country partnership strategy; DMC = developing member country; DOC = Department of Communications; ERCD = Economic Research and Regional Cooperation; FCAS = fragile and conflict-affected situations; KAA = key action area; PPFD = Procurement, Portfolio and Financial Management Department; PSOD = Private Sector Operations Department; Q = quarter; RD = regional department; SA = sub-action; SDCC = Sustainable Development and Climate Change Department; SIDS = small island developing states; SPD = Strategy, Policy, and Partnerships Department.

Source: Asian Development Bank.

Appendix 6

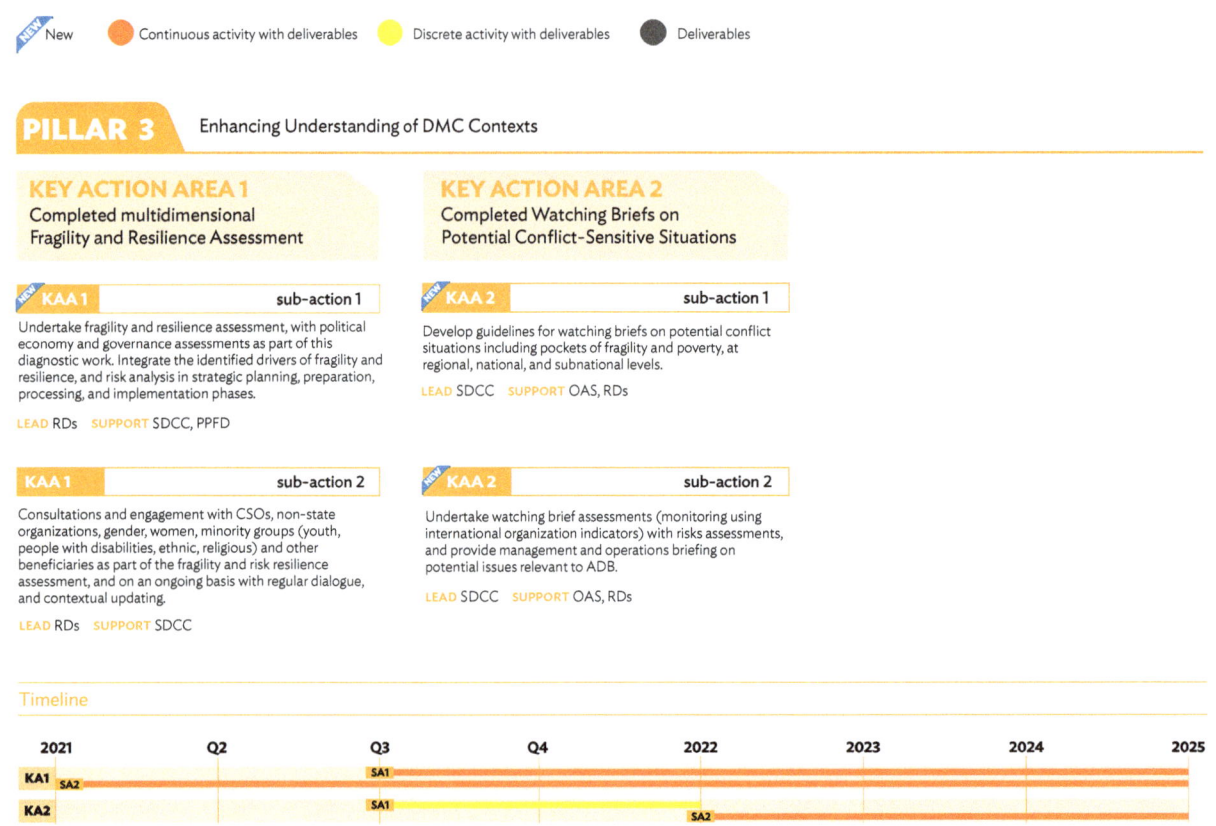

ADB = Asian Development Bank; ADF = Asian Development Fund; BPMSD = Budget, People, and Management Systems Department; COBP = country operations business plan; CSO = civil society organization; DMC = developing member country; FCAS = fragile and conflict-affected situations; KAA = key action area; OAS = Office of Administrative Services; PPFD = Procurement, Portfolio, and Financial Management Department; Q = quarter; RD = regional department; SA = sub-action; SDCC = Sustainable Development and Climate Change Department; SIDS = small island developing states.

Source: Asian Development Bank.

The fragile and conflict-affected situations (FCAS) and small island developing states (SIDS) approach (FSA) Action Plan is built on three pillars to improve the performance of the Asian Development Bank (ADB) in FCAS and SIDS, and help developing member countries (DMCs) achieve better development outcomes and their Sustainable Development Goals (SDGs) targets. The three pillars are outlined below with planned key action areas and detailed sub-actions.

Pillar 1: Improving Responsiveness of Standard ADB Processes, Procedures, and Practices for FCAS and SIDS Differentiated Approaches

Key sub-actions under the FSA Action Plan will build on existing ADB initiatives, develop new and revised processes and procedures as part of an integrated approach to improving operational effectiveness in FCAS and SIDS contexts. This will be achieved through sub-actions in five key action areas (KAAs):

KAA 1: Adoption of risk-based strategic planning and business processes. Core sub-actions in this KAA will involve

(i) Integrating the fragility and resilience assessment (FRA) contextual analysis findings on critical drivers of fragility and resilience options into the diagnostic work as part of the risk-based country partnership strategy programming, and into project preparation and design. Ongoing contextual changes to be monitored and integrated in the country operations business plan and project reviews.

(ii) Introducing new and revamped business processes, procedures, and guidelines that incorporate both flexibility and enhancements for FCAS and SIDS settings. This will involve actions to update staff instructions for FCAS and SIDS operations, participate in and conduct reviews of business processes and the procurement frameworks for FCAS and SIDS environments, use of differentiated performance targets, and other aspects of project processing and implementation. The sub-action will also involve engagement in thematic analyses reviews, such as for environmental and social risk management and safeguards, climate change and disaster risk management, gender, poverty, and social dimension. A complementary action is to provide staff with stronger technical support and guidance to clarify flexibilities in existing business processes and procedures, and to support counterpart DMCs in these areas.

(iii) Streamline business processes to (a) support an increased uptake of private sector investments, especially small nonsovereign transactions in SIDS and FCAS, and review business processes with a focus on the Faster Approach to Small Nonsovereign Transactions; and (b) allow for flexibility with risk premium pricing on such loans and supportive sovereign technical assistance grants.

(iv) Providing technical support to improve the use and adoption of flexibilities under existing business processes and procedures.

KAA 2: FCAS- and SIDS-responsive project modalities in operational use. Core sub-actions in this KAA will involve

(i) Increasing the use of diversified products, instruments, and funding modalities for sovereign operations in DMCs designated as FCAS or SIDS. In SIDS, this may involve expanded use of contingent disaster funding in the context of disaster risk management, and programming approaches involving policy-based lending for public sector reforms. In addition to adapting and modifying traditional project financing modalities, and blended financing options, the focus is on how flexibility can be enhanced to respond to the contextual environment and risk changes, with elements of adaptive financing introduced under ADB funding modalities.

(ii) Increasing uptake of smaller nonsovereign transactions, which includes measures to enhance flexibility and risk sharing of credit enhancement and other products.

KAA 3: Context-appropriate project preparation, design, and implementation procedures. Core sub-actions in this KAA will involve

(i) Integrating FRA findings and resilience actions for the specific sector and locational context into the project concept stage (as part of the initial poverty and social analysis, and the environmental and social risk classification of projects)[1] and in project preparation and design.

(ii) Increasing the use of project readiness financing and small expenditure financing facilities to enhance project readiness, especially of larger infrastructure projects.

(iii) Increasing the use and adoption of alternative and innovative project design and implementation arrangements, and enhancing

---

[1] To be further developed through ADB's Safeguard Policy Statement update.

project supervision and implementation, strategic procurement planning, and (if identified as required) stronger ADB support and engagement mechanisms to address critical constraints, such as those related to the delivery of environmental and social mitigation measures in projects.
(iv) Undertaking capacity assessments of executing and implementing agencies, based on existing capacities, and developing realistic support plans that are incorporated into the project design. This may include capacity assessments and support plans to environmental and land management agencies to address and reduce potential safeguard risks and delays.

KAA 4: Integration of digital technologies. The core sub-action in this KAA will involve

(i) Supporting development and integration of digital technologies appropriate for FCAS and SIDS contexts (for preparation, implementation, and monitoring) and establishing integrated digital databases. This would be as part of ADB's digital agenda and knowledge management action plan. The digital technologies would support increased uptake and better capability to perform remote sensing, geospatial mapping, and independent third-party monitoring, which are necessary in geographical areas in DMCs where ADB operations face conflicts, remoteness, or low density of population and infrastructure. Also, it would provide the potential for assessing population displacement and other social impacts, environmental damage, and marine and climate change resilience.

KAA 5: FCAS- and SIDS-responsive monitoring and reporting systems operational. Core sub-actions in this KAA will involve the Sustainable Development and Climate Change Department FCAS team taking the lead in:

(i) Developing the methodology and performance standards in FCAS and SIDS results and monitoring frameworks at country program and project level.
(ii) Developing and maintaining a dedicated dashboard that includes reporting on key performance indicators.
(iii) Preparing an annual FSA report to Management on FSA achievements, FSA adoption, and performance; and undertaking a midterm review in 2023, and an evaluation at the end of the FSA in 2025.

Pillar 2: Increasing ADB's Institutional Capacity for Operations in FCAS and SIDS

Implementing the FSA plan will require increasing ADB's institutional capacity for operations in FCAS and SIDS, at strategic and operational levels, to enable the cultural and behavioral changes associated with the adoption of a differentiated approach, ownership by operational departments, and adequate staffing with skilled personnel to provide the necessary in-field and hands-on technical and operational presence. This will be achieved through actions in six KAAs:

KAA 1: Enhanced ADB's organizational coordination of operations in FCAS and SIDS. Core sub-actions in this KAA will involve

(i) Providing adequate staff (with the required mix of skills and expertise) and resources for the FCAS team to undertake FSA functions, including application of the FCAS lens in key areas of operations (themes, sectors, and compliance).
(ii) Formalizing FCAS and SIDS working groups, terms of reference and objectives, and for FCAS and SIDS participation in policy, planning (including FRA and CPS preparation), in operational priority areas, and related networks across sector and thematic groups.
(iii) Supporting the FCAS anchors and designated staff focal points across regional departments; resident missions and field offices; supporting departments; technical

divisions (procurement, controllers, financial management, general counsel, and safeguards); and sector and thematic groups.
(iv) Preparing technical assistance projects for DMCs to ensure adequate and consistent support to FCAS and SIDS operations. This will include innovative use of technologies and training based on DMC-specific needs analyses.
(v) Developing and implementing a comprehensive communication strategy, with plans and tools to be prepared to facilitate and promote FCAS understanding and knowledge of best practices by both ADB staff across the organization, and by external stakeholders in DMCs, civil society, and development partners.

KAA 2: Strengthened knowledge and analytics. Core sub-actions in this KAA will involve

(i) Developing data visualization analytics and tools to support analysis and classification of geographically specific fragility, poverty, conflict, climate change and disaster risk management parameters, and other parameters, including for DMCs classification.[2]
(ii) Strengthening ADB's FCAS and SIDS analytics and knowledge products, based on a needs assessment, and enhancing knowledge management and transfer using ADB knowledge networks.

KAA 3: ADB staff more effective in applying contextual knowledge of FCAS and SIDS and associated skills. Core sub-actions in this KAA will involve

(i) (a) developing a competency framework; (b) preparing new or adapted, differentiated, and strengthened training courses and materials that will be applicable in FCAS and SIDS contexts (based on the training needs analysis) to support assessments, processing, and implementing operations; (c) developing and supporting a peer-to-peer mentoring training program; and (d) undertaking a survey and identifying ADB-wide expertise in relevant countries or sectors or themes for FCAS and SIDS contexts.
(ii) Developing and delivering FCAS- and SIDS-specific training modules for staff assigned to work in FCAS and SIDS contexts (Asian Development Fund 13 commitment), and in ADB induction program basic training modules.
(iii) Training ADB staff in institutional capacity development approaches to address contextual and institutional capacity deficits in FCAS and SIDS, identifying feasible alternatives when building capacity and sustainability to deliver government functions, and in the transition toward resilience.

KAA 4: Enhanced ADB responsiveness. Core sub-actions in this KAA will involve

(i) Strengthening ADB's field presence (based on needs as assessed by the regional departments) through staff training and repurposing of vacant staff positions, pooling cross-regional expertise, and attracting experienced and motivated staff and/or experienced FCAS and SIDS consultants. Based on the identified needs, increasing ADB technical expert support (sector, implementation, procurement, financial management, and safeguard experts).
(ii) Developing contextual terms of reference to attract experienced and motivated staff and/or consultants, and applying specific recruitment strategies for international and national consultants with FCAS and SIDS experience.

---

[2] This could include earth observation, or intelligent systems for monitoring, control, and diagnosis of process systems as artificial intelligence, and network analysis to assess multiple and growing parameters, generating a dynamic 360° map of the environment.

KAA 5: Stronger human resource policies and enhanced incentives. Core sub-actions in this KAA will involve

(i) Applying effective incentive structures (financial and nonfinancial) to attract and retain skilled staff in FCAS and SIDS, raising awareness of incentive schemes, and promoting the recruitment and transfer of competent and motivated staff.
(ii) Encouraging national FCAS and SIDS staff to uptake short-term assignments to promote context exposure and awareness among sectors and regions and develop a talent pool of FCAS and SIDS experts.

KAA 6: Expanded partnerships and coordination. Core sub-actions in this KAA will involve

(i) Expanding global, regional, and country-specific partnerships and engagement for analytics and knowledge sharing, training, capacity building, and joint assessment work in DMCs.
(ii) Increasing national coordination with DMCs and development partners on joint programming, funding, and cofinancing opportunities. In conflict DMCs, participating in humanitarian development–peacebuilding forums.

Pillar 3: Enhancing Understanding of DMC Contexts

Implementing the FSA plan will require a detailed understanding on the specific DMC contextual constraints, and the causes of the increasing fragility at regional, national, subnational and local levels, across FCAS, SIDS, and context-sensitive situations. This will be achieved through sub-actions in two KAAs:

KAA 1: Completed multidimensional fragility and resilience assessments. Core sub-actions in this KAA will involve

(i) Undertaking FRA that include political economy and governance assessments; and integrating the identified drivers of fragility and resilience, and the risk analysis in strategic planning and programming, and in project preparation, processing, and implementation.
(ii) Carrying out consultations and engaging with civil society organizations; other non-state organizations; women's groups; minority groups such as youth, people with disabilities, ethnic groups, indigenous people's organizations;[3] and beneficiaries as part of the FRA, and on an ongoing basis with regular dialogue and contextual updates.

KAA 2: Completed watching briefs on potential conflict-sensitive situations. Core sub-actions in this KAA will involve

(i) Developing guidelines for watching briefs on potential context-sensitive situations, including pockets of fragility and poverty, at regional (including transboundary flashpoints), national, and subnational levels.
(ii) Undertaking watching brief assessments (monitoring using international organization indicators) with risk assessments, and providing management and operations briefings on potential issues relevant to ADB.

---

[3] Stakeholders include all the most vulnerable groups, such as the poor, women, all sexual orientation and gender identities, indigenous peoples, ethnic minorities, persons with disabilities, hard-to-reach and remote populations, migrants, displaced, and conflict-affected people.

APPENDIX 7
Business Process and Procedure Reform

This appendix summarizes priority changes of business processes and procedures to strengthen guidance on and support for Asian Development Bank (ADB) operations in in fragile and conflict-affected situations (FCAS) and small island developing states (SIDS) settings. These changes are aligned and reinforced by corporate initiatives that cover organizational realignment, institutional changes, and capacity development, strengthening of resident mission and field office operations, and the implementation of ADB's digital agenda. Table A7.1 presents the identified changes of business processes, procedures, and guidelines; the status of ongoing efforts and actions, if any; and the links to the pillars and key result areas of the in FCAS and SIDS approach Action Plan, 2021–2025. For each proposed change, remarks provide context, background, and further clarity.

Table A7.2 provides the same level of information, but related to sector and project-level.

Supplementary Appendix 2 (available upon request) provides a detailed listing of FCAS and SIDS-related ADB business processes, procedures, and guidelines.

Table A7.1: ADB Country-Level Business Processes, Procedures, and Guidelines Changes

#	Area of Change	Business Process/ Guidance Support	Status/ Ongoing Efforts (✓)	FSA Pillars and Key Action Area	Remarks
	Country Level				
1	Strengthened diagnostics to inform CPS preparation: - FRA (including PEA) - GRA	Revised OM SI GN New templates	✓	Ongoing with expected completion Q4 2021 **Lead:** SPD, SDCC **Support:** RDs	Pillar 1 - KAA 1	For FCAS and SIDS, this is intended to integrate FRA findings into ADB operations on a systematic basis.
2	Review of Safeguard Policy Statement (SPS), related procedures along with enhanced guidance and support	Update of SPS (policy) Revised OM GN	✓	Ongoing with expected completion in Q3 2022 **Lead:** SDCC **Support:** ODs, SPD	Pillar 1 - KAA 1	Involves use of risk-based tools at country or sector level to enhance safeguards planning, preparatory work, and implementation.
3	CSO operations	New SI GN	✓	Ongoing with expected completion in Q4 2021 **Lead:** SDCC **Support:** ODs, SPD	Pillar 1 - KAA 1	Expanded CSO consultations at country and project level to enhance relevance and responsiveness of ADB operations.
4	Revised FCAS classification system	SPD memo	✓	Under review SDCC **Lead:** SDCC, SPD **Support:** SPD, ERCD	Pillar 2 - KAA 2	A revised evidence-based FCAS classification that reflects regional dimensions and SIDS characteristics.

ADB = Asian Development Bank, CPS = country partnership strategy, CSO = civil society organization, ERCD = Economic Research and Regional Cooperation Department, FCAS = fragile and conflict-affected situations, FRA = fragility and resilience assessment, FSA = FCAS and SIDS Approach, GN = guidance note, GRA = governance risk assessment, KAA = key action area, OD = operations department, OM = Operations Manual, PEA = political economy assessment, Q = quarter, RD = regional department, SDCC = Sustainable Development and Climate Change Department, SI = staff instruction, SIDS = small island developing states, SPD = Strategy, Policy, and Partnerships Department.

Source: Asian Development Bank.

Table A7.2: ADB Sector- or Project-Level Business Processes, Procedures, and Guidelines Changes

#	Area of Change	Business Process/ Guidance Support	Status/ Ongoing Efforts (✓)	FSA Pillars and Key Action Area	Remarks
Sector or Project Level					
5	Integrating existing procedural flexibility to improve processing efficiency of sovereign grants and loans in FCAS and SIDS	Updated SI GN	Under discussion **Lead:** SPD **Support:** SDCC, ODs	Pillar 1 - KAA 1	To support FSA institutionalization and operationalization the review of updated relevant supporting documents is discussed to include flexibility in project processing and implementation including performance monitoring.
6	Enhanced guidance and support in procurement and financial management	Updated guidelines	Under discussion **Lead:** PPFD **Support:** ODs, SDCC	Pillar 1 - KAA 1	The focus is to expand guidance on procurement in fragile, conflict-affected, and emergency situations and include SIDS. Review of procedures and guidance on financial management.
7	Streamlined processing of small NSO transactions under special FAST procedures	Updated SI (based on paper to be submitted to the Board in Q2 2021)	✓ Ongoing with expected completion in Q4 2021 **Lead:** SPD, PSOD **Support:** OGC, ODs	Pillar 1 - KAA 1	Includes various measures that will support enhanced PSO in FCAS and SIDS.
8	Project preparation and design including FRA findings based on sector or local context	RRP Linked Document	Under discussion **Lead:** SDCC **Support:** ODs	Pillar 1 - KAA 1	FRA findings to be fully incorporated into project design and processing requirements.
9	Detailed capacity assessment and support plan	RRP Annex, Assessment	Under discussion **Lead:** ODs **Support:** SDCC	Pillar 1- KAA 1	Based on FCAS/SIDS context and identified needs, adopted at departmental level.
10	PAM to capture in greater detail implementation arrangements to facilitate responsiveness to local context	RRP Annex, Template	Under discussion **Lead:** ODs **Support:** PPFD, SDCC	Pillar 1- KAA 1	Tailored PAM to be adopted at departmental level.
11	Development and integration of digital technologies for FCAS and SIDS settings	GN	Under discussion **Lead:** SDCC **Support:** ODs	Pillar 1- KAA 1	Introduction of relevant digital technologies, supporting DMC and project performance monitoring including third-party independent monitoring.

ADB = Asian Development Bank; CPS = country partnership strategy; DMC = developing member country; FAST = Faster Approach to Small Nonsovereign Transactions; FCAS = fragile and conflict-affected situations; FRA = fragility and resilience assessment; FSA = FCAS and SIDS Approach; GN = guidance note; GRA = governance risk assessment; ISGA = inclusive and sustainable growth assessment; KAA = key action area; NSO = nonsovereign operations; OD = operations department; OGC = Office of the General Counsel; OM = Operations Manual; PAM = Project Administration Manual; PPFD = Procurement, Portfolio, and Financial Department; PSO = private sector operations; PSOD = Private Sector Operations Department; Q = quarter; RD = regional department; RRP = report and recommendation of the President; SDCC = Sustainable Development and Climate Change Department; SI = staff instruction; SIDS = small island developing states; SPD = Strategy, Policy, and Partnerships Department.

Source: Asian Development Bank.

APPENDIX 8
FCAS and SIDS Approach Results Framework

SUSTAINABLE DEVELOPMENT

1. Improved livelihoods, inclusiveness, and resilience in FCAS and SIDS

   1.A. Applicable seven operational priority areas results disaggregated by FCAS and SIDS (New)

2. Improved performance of ADB operations in FCAS and SIDS

   2.A. Clients in FCAS and SIDS satisfied with ADB's development effectiveness (%) (CRF-TI)
   2.B. Clients in FCAS and SIDS satisfied with the use of ADB knowledge products (%) (CRF-RFI)
   2.C. Clients in FCAS and SIDS satisfied with ADB's responsiveness in helping them achieve results (%) (CRF-TI)
   2.D. Client rating on efficiency of ADB's delivery of TA in FCAS and SIDS (%) (New)
   2.E. Completed operations rated successful (%, SOV):
      a. Projects   c. FCAS DMCs
      b. PBL   d. SIDS (CRF-TI)
   2.F. Completed operations rated successful (%, NSO):
      a. Development results   c. ADB's work quality (CRF-TI)
      b. ADB's additionality
   2.G. Operations including meaningful civil society organizations engagement (%) (sovereign)

3. Increased use of differentiated approaches in ADB operations in FCAS and SIDS

   3.A. Performance of sovereign operations at implementation in FCAS and SIDS rated satisfactory (%) (CRF-RFI)
   3.B. FCAS and SIDS nonsovereign operations at risk of not achieving development results (%) (CRF-RFI)
   3.C. Operations integrating differentiated approaches (adaptiveness, responsiveness, etc.) throughout the project cycle (%) (New)
   3.D. Commitments in FCAS and SIDS (%, SOV and NSO) (CRF-TI)
   3.E. Staff reporting improved knowledge, understanding and use of the differentiated approaches (%) (New)
   3.F. Client rating on alignment of ADB's technical assistance operations with DMC national development priorities (%) (New)

PILLAR 1
Improving responsiveness of standard ADB processes and procedures for FCAS and SIDS differentiated approaches

ACTION TRACKER

PILLAR 2
Increasing ADB FCAS and SIDS institutional capacity

2.1. Budgeted international and national staff positions in FCAS and SIDS field offices (CRF-TI)
2.2. Sovereign operations administered in field offices in FCAS and SIDS (%) (CRF-TI)

ACTION TRACKER

PILLAR 3
Improving DMCs contextual analysis and understanding by ADB

3.1. FCAS and SIDS specific knowledge products and services delivered (%) (CRF-TI)
3.2. Stakeholders and beneficiaries satisfied with ADB's collaboration with development partners in FCAS and SIDS (%) (CRF-TI)

ACTION TRACKER

MEASURING RESULTS
18 Indicators
- CRF indicators: 13
- New indicators: 5
- Data source:
  - Client Survey
  - Staff Survey
  - Administrative Data

ACTION TRACKER
13 Key action area
34 Sub-actions

Each sub-action in the action plan will be regularly reviewed for continued relevance. This could include adding, modifying, or discontinuing actions. The status of the sub-actions and the implementation metrics will be supplemented by a description of the action's progress and of the measures taken.

The action tracker will be reported yearly.

Action Tracker Dashboard

Serial No.	Sub-action No.	Item	Implementation Lead - Support	Completion date	Status	Progress	Justification/Notes
					- Ongoing - Modified - Discontinued - New	FI - fully implemented LI - largely implemented PI - partly implemented NI - not implemented	

ADB = Asian Development Bank, CRF = corporate results framework, DMC = developing member country, FCAS = fragile and conflict-affected situations, NSO = nonsovereign operations, PBL = policy-based lending, RFI = results framework indicator, SIDS = small island developing states, SOV = sovereign operations, TA = technical assistance, TI = tracking indicator.

Source: Asian Development Bank.